Hagbard Brase

Beloved Music Master

HAGBARD BRASE, 1877–1953
Portrait by Dale Hoag

Hagbard Brase

Beloved Music Master

By Emory Lindquist

Emory Lindquist

Bethany College Press
Lindsborg, Kansas

Bethany College Press
Lindsborg, Kansas 67456
A. John Pearson, Editor

HAGBARD BRASE: BELOVED MUSIC MASTER

First Edition
ISBN 0-916030-06-7
Library of Congress Catalog Card Number 84-16773

Library of Congress Cataloging in Publication Data

Lindquist, Emory Kempton, 1908-
  Hagbard Brase: beloved music master

  Bibliography: p.
  1. Brase, Hagbard, 1877-1953.   2. Conductors (Music)—United States—
Biography. I. Title.
ML422.B8L5   1984   784.1'0092'4 [B]   84-16773
ISBN 0-916030-06-7

THE MESSIAH

*(To Dr. Hagbard Brase and the Bethany Oratorio Society,
Lindsborg, Kansas, April 22, 1946)*

Once more the stone is rolled away
From the Easter sepulchre;
Again the miracle of Resurrection Day
Resounds across the world
In music like a mighty paean
Of praise unfurled
In vast wings of sound.
Blighted and frustrated humanity
Lifts its weary head and drinks new faith
From the message of immortality
Climaxing in the fervor
Of a rapturous Hallelujah
And the infinite thunder
Of a triumphant Amen.

Jessie Lofgren Kraft
Overtone, page 63

Dedicated
to the members of the Bethany College Oratorio Society
who shared with Hagbard Brase in the great Lindsborg
oratorio tradition.

PREFACE AND ACKNOWLEDGEMENTS

The life and career of Hagbard Brase, famous oratorio society conductor, teacher, organist and composer at Bethany College for more than half a century, provides another fine example of the legacy that talented and dedicated sons and daughters of Europe have contributed to American life. The New World offered challenges and opportunities to which he responded with gratifying results.

Following studies at Skara School and the Royal Conservatory of Music, Stockholm, Hagbard Brase emigrated to Lindsborg, Kansas, in 1900. Although the young man in his early twenties found himself in a milieu quite different from that of Skara and Stockholm in Sweden, his fine personal qualities and talent were soon recognized and appreciated. He began a career at Bethany College which lasted as long as life itself.

Paramount in Hagbard Brase's life work was his distinguished service to the Bethany College Oratorio Society, often referred to as the Lindsborg "Messiah Chorus." He was organist from 1900 to 1914 and then director for more than three decades until retirement in 1946. A music critic described his achievement during those years in the following words: "To Dr. Brase's splendid musical training and ideals the oratorio society owes its rank among the first choruses of the world."

Hagbard Brase was also an inspiring teacher, a fine organist and a talented composer. This beloved music master was a man of keen intelligence, true sensitivity, broad culture and high ideals. Hagbard Brase was a deeply religious man who shared firm but quiet views of life's greatest values. Although he never lost the distinctive qualities of his European background, he fully understood the problems and aspirations of his new homeland. He was an unforgettable person who generated esteem and respect. Family, friends, and admirers in large numbers hold him in kindly remembrance.

The papers of Hagbard Brase provide rewarding sources for study. Included are letters to and from members of his family, friends and associates in Sweden and America; lectures on conducting an oratorio chorus, the meaning of Bach's *The Passion of Our Lord According to St. Matthew*, the origin, development and importance of church music; and an intimate description of vital religious experience. The prin-

cipal source in the Brase papers is his remembrances of the years
which he recorded for his family in 1945 in the form of "Memoirs."
Extensive excerpts from these materials are used in this volume.

The life of Hagbard Brase was immensely enriched through a fine
family. Only one year passed between the arrival of Brase in Lindsborg and his marriage there to Minna Hernwall, Halmstad, his Swedish fiancé. They shared the problems of adaptation to the new milieu,
which at times resulted in acute longing for home (*hemlängtan*). The
future assumed new dimensions of interest and meaning as the family
circle included five children—Thorborg, Karin, Yngve, Sonja and Ingrid. These resources were expanded and enriched with the passing
of the years and the addition of spouses and grandchildren. In the
twilight years of life there was a sense of belonging to the future for
Hagbard and Minna Brase.

In the context of the above factors the research and writing of this
volume was a pleasant and gratifying experience. In addition to the
availability of extensive Brase family papers, generous responses to
interviews by members of the family greatly enriched the sources of
information. Kenneth W. Willey, a son-in-law of Hagbard and Minna
Brase, was an especially vital force in initiating and developing this
biography.

Several persons in Sweden provided helpful guidance and infor-
mation. Included among them are *Rektor* Arne Palmqvist, Skara School,
Rektor Harald Ryfors, Göteborg, a nephew of Hagbard Brase, *Fil. lic.*
Ola Christensson, a librarian at Göteborg University and Karin Stenfors, Stockholm. Dixie Lanning, Librarian of Bethany College and Dr.
Eugene Holdsworth, Music Department Head, assisted in various ways.
Eighteen former Brase students presented at my request valuable
"Remembrances of Hagbard Brase." Their names are cited in the text
where they are quoted. Carol N. Anderson, Bethany graduate and well-
known Kansas choral conductor, urged me in the first instance to write
this biography.

I am thankful for the fine assistance of two former students of Dr.
Brase. Neloise Hodges Stapp is a graduate of Bethany College and
a former member of the music faculty. Lambert Dahlsten, also a
Bethany alumnus and Emeritus Professor of Piano and Organ, is
the organist for the Oratorio Society, a position which he has held
with distinction for more than three decades. They have not only provided valuable understanding of their former teacher, but they have
read and discussed the manuscript with me, thus eliminating errors
and enriching the contents. I also greatly appreciate the helpful sug-
gestions made by Dr. Delmar C. Homan, the Margaret H. Mountcastle
Distinguished Professor of Humanities at Bethany College.

Lauran Elmquist Lofgren and Jane Asche at Bethany College prepared the manuscript for publication with great skill and understanding. I thank both of them for their fine service.

The dedicatory poem by Jessie Lofgren Kraft, "The Messiah," was first published in *Overtone* by Exposition Press, New York, 1947, and it is reprinted with permission.

It is a pleasure to have this volume published by the Bethany College Press. In this relationship and others, I am grateful to Dr. Peter Ristuben, President of Bethany College, for his personal interest and support. Finally, I express hearty appreciation to A. John Pearson, Director of Public Relations, Bethany College, who has been a wise adviser and a knowledgeable editor.

The pages that follow are designed to describe the main aspects of the life and contribution of Hagbard Brase whose gracious spirit and distinguished achievement have provided a precious legacy for succeeding generations. Errors and omissions are the responsibility of the author.

Table of Contents

The Bethany College Oratorio Society is pictured in 1915 in the old Ling Auditorium on the campus of Bethany College, during the first year under direction of Dr. Hagbard Brase. The soloists for that year's Festival were soprano Ethyl Coover, alto Ida Gardner, tenor Arvid Wallin, and bass Thure Jaderborg. All but Gardner were members of the Bethany College faculty. At various times Ling Auditorium was also called Bethany College Auditorium and the "Messiah" auditorium. The building was constructed in 1895 and was destroyed by fire in 1946. During that time it was the home of Messiah and other oratorios, as well as the famous Messiah Festival, until Presser Hall auditorium became available in the fall of 1928.

Dr. Brase (center) poses in 1942 in Presser Hall auditorium with the chorus and orchestra of the Bethany College Oratorio Society. Soloists that year were soprano Hilda Ohlin, alto Ellen Repp, tenor Hubert Norville, and bass Foster Miller. In the history of the society, Dr. Brase's tenure as conductor is unsurpassed in length of service—as he served from 1915 until his retirement following the 1946 season. He had joined the College faculty in 1900; he became the organ accompanist in 1901; and he assumed the position of conductor in 1915. His fine general musicianship and his understanding of the oratorio tradition at Bethany were of great importance in his long record of achievement—which included service as teacher, composer, organist, and conductor.

I.

The Early Years in Sweden

In the parish of Råda, south of Lake Vänern in the Lidköping area of beautiful Västergötland, Hagbard Brase was born on September 25, 1877. His parents were *Komminister* (assistant pastor) Johannes and Lydia Carolina Jungner Brase. A daughter, Ingegerd, had been born in April of the previous year. The family lived in the church property named Braddegården, which had been the residence of Råda *komministers* since 1682. It was located on the edge of the range where the road from famous Läckö castle climbs up a mighty morainic slope. On three sides a large area of forest provided a pleasing view. The other side opened to a fertile and productive valley.

Hagbard's paternal family traced its origin to the farm, *Bragnum*, near the parish of Lekåsa, about forty miles from Råda. His grandfather, Andreas Andersson, a tailor, and his wife, Annika Andersson, were from Lekåsa. The great grandfather, a soldier in the provincial army (lantvarnet), had received the name *Bra* (good), a so-called *soldatnamn* (soldier's name) often assigned during compulsory military training service to avoid difficulties caused by the multitude of patronymic names like Andersson and Johansson. Hagbard's father had planned to adopt the name Braeson (son of *Bra*), but as Hagbard has explained, Pastor Sandgren of Bitterna suggested the name Brase, which was accepted.[1]

When Hagbard's father, *Komminister* Johannes Brase, married Lydia Carolina Jungner at Levene, the young clergyman entered a family that traced its origin directly to Torde Bonde, a privy councillor (riksråd), who died in 1329. The Jungner name has its origin in the parish of Jung, Västergötland, and was adopted by Jonas, son of Bryngal Larsson and Elisabeth Haraldsdotter, who had married Christina Florén. Their son *Kyrkoherde* (Dean) Johan Jungner, married Caro-

lina Lovisa Lundblad, who were the parents of Lydia Carolina Jungner, Hagbard Brase's mother. There were many Lutheran pastors in
the Jungner and Lundblad families.[2]

Johannes Brase was a talented boy who early showed great interest
in reading and learning. Lindsborg pastor and historian, the late Dr.
Alfred Bergin, who grew up in that area of Sweden, had heard about
Johannes reading a book as the youth worked in his father's tailor
shop at Bitterna. Since educational opportunities were limited and
work at an early age was normal for sons, young Brase enrolled in
Skara läroverk (Skara School) in 1861 at an older age than most students. He qualified for the certificate authorizing enrollment in a university (*studenten*) in less than the usual time. In 1869 he entered
Uppsala University where he was a member of the student society of
Västergötland (*Västgöta Nationsförening*). He completed theological
studies at Uppsala leading to ordination as a pastor in the Church of
Sweden in 1871. He became *Komminister* (assistant pastor) in 1873
at Råda, which traces its origin to the twelfth century.[3]

While visiting in Levene, the young pastor met Lydia Carolina

*An artist's sketch of the Lutheran church at Råda. Here Hagbard Brase's father, Jo-
hannes Brase, was the pastor when Hagbard was born in 1877 and when his sister,
Ingegerd, was born the previous year.*

Jungner, daughter of *Kyrkoherde* and *Fru* Johan Jungner. They were married there April 21, 1875. Lydia Carolina was in frail health and it was necessary for her to be seated during the marriage ceremony. However, she made a fine home for her husband and their children, Ingegerd and Hagbard.[4]

Komminister Johannes Brase was highly esteemed by members of the Råda parish. He has been described as "combining keen fortitude with earnest piety and a fine pastoral spirit; he was a good preacher, a zealous shepherd of souls, energetic and practical. Tracing his ancestry to the common people, he understood them and they understood him."[5]

Hagbard's father enjoyed working on the church land. His rural constituents were impressed by their young pastor who worked with spade and hoe in his spare time and during vacations. His energetic sister, Maja-Stina, worked with him occasionally in preparing moss land for arable fields. He succeeded within a few years in doubling the tillable land allocated to him as partial compensation for his services as pastor.[6]

This extra physical activity was carried on while devoting himself faithfully to the preaching and teaching ministry of the church. His duties were so pressing that his wife, Lydia, wrote to her parents expressing deep regret that they could not attend her father's fiftieth ordination anniversary. It was necessary for *Komminister* Brase to be in Råda in order to present a report to the supervising pastor of the area.[7]

Brase took seriously the assignment of conducting regular meetings at the homes of parish members when an opportunity was made available for them to demonstrate their knowledge of the Bible and Martin Luther's *Catechism* and receive counseling and instruction from their pastor (husförhör). Following a series of these meetings in extremely cold weather, Johannes Brase was stricken with pneumonia which caused his death on November 25, 1879, at the age of thirty-six. His wife, although in frail health, survived him twenty years.[8]

After Johannes Brase's death, the family moved to Levene and lived in one of two attached wings of the large *prästgård* (rectory) of the Jungners, the parents of Hagbard's mother. Hagbard's only playmate was Ingegerd, his sister. He had good relations with the hired men. One of them made a small wagon for him, and when it was broken, he recalled dragging it along a path in the forest to the hut of an old man who promised to fix it. Hagbard remembered across the years the large residence of the pastor's family, surrounded by a garden with old fruit trees. There was also a small lake, a garden house, a bridge to an island, a perfect setting for a romance in the romantic period of

The birthplace of Hagbard Brase at Råda was in the beautiful Swedish province of Västergötland. Here Johannes and Lydia Brase lived with their two children, Hagbard and Ingegerd, until Johannes died from pneumonia when Hagbard was two years old.

A modern-day view of the Råda Church.

more than a century ago. Hagbard remembered the old church at Levene. The front door had many bullet holes from the wars with the Danes in the Middle Ages and later. He visited the "Hill of Håkan the Red," an early king or chief, who supposedly was buried there.[9]

Hagbard was five years old when Grandfather Jungner died in 1883. He remembered that there were many people at the funeral, among them military officers in uniform. Sister Ingegerd and he thought they were kings. "There comes another king, we whispered to each other as we peered through a half-open door."[10]

Hagbard's mother, grandmother, sister Ingegerd, *Faster* (paternal aunt) Maja-Stina and he moved to Skara to add further to Uncle Ernst Jungner's large household. Their residence adjoined that of Uncle Ernst and was called *Paradiset* (Paradise). Girl roomers, who attended Uncle Ernst's private school, lived there during the academic year. Hagbard had several friends in the area including Nils Petersson, who, when he grew up, changed his name to Schenke, and became a well-known educator and public official. Another friend, Samuel Landtmanson, whose father *Fil. dr.* (doctor of philosophy) Carl Johan Gustaf Landtmanson, a teacher at *Skara läroverk*, lived across the street. This friend became *rektor* (president) of *Västerås läroverk* (Västerås School).[11]

The home where Hagbard lived in Levene with his widowed mother and his sister, Ingegerd.

ABOVE, LEFT: Rev. Johannes Brase, Hagbard's father.

ABOVE, RIGHT: Lydia Carolina Brase, Hagbard's mother.

RIGHT: Hagbard and Ingegerd Brase.

At the age of four Hagbard became a pupil in the model school which was associated with Uncle Ernst's seminary for girls. He completed four classes in this school, and in 1888 he enrolled in *Skara läroverk*. He was a student there until 1895.[12] When ten year-old Hagbard Brase entered this fine school in the autumn of 1888, he became part of a tradition that began in August 1641, when Queen Christina authorized the founding of a *gymnasium* (upper school) at Skara. Instruction had begun the following year.[13]

Hagbard Brase, in his "Memoirs," has provided a description of those early years at *Skara läroverk*: "School started at 6:30 a.m. Imagine a little boy of ten struggling through two feet of snow at 6:15 a.m. in a pitch dark morning on his way to school. Chapel services were held at 6:30 a.m. when we sang, "The Bright Sun Goes Up Again" (*Den klara sol går åter upp*) two hours before it did. Here is the schedule: Classes from 7–9, breakfast and home study, 9–10:30, classes 11–12 and again at 5:00 p.m. Saturday was a school day like every other day except Sunday."[14]

One cold November Hagbard and two of his friends watched as workmen put up a statue of the Virgin Mary above the door on the side of the cathedral opposite the school. One of the Latin teachers, Johan Hjerten, who had responsibility for renovating the cathedral, told the boys as they stood there watching the workmen: "Remember that you were present when this statue was hoisted into place." Brase wrote a half century or more later: "I have remembered it." His large postcard collection of Skara scenes and sites contains a reproduction of this statue of the Virgin Mary.[15]

Hagbard Brase has written that "The new college subjects interested me at first but I soon lost interest. I understand now that I was impatient... When I was supposed to study Caesar or the *Metamorphoses* of Ovid, I translated *Livy* instead. I had bought one of his books at an auction. I remember how much I liked his book. Greek was of great interest to me. The teacher was a very learned man, he explained the lesson, then told us to study it while he pulled a magazine from his pocket and read for the rest of the hour." The young student was impressed with his teachers. The Latin teacher was Per Gustaf Petterson, "Latin Pelle"; Johan Edward Torell, "Klotsen," taught history; the instructor in chemistry, Anders J. Sahlen was known as "Floten"—all had interesting names which the pupils used. Other teachers included Anders Nilsson, history, who was a collector of archaeological and historical items, described as "Skara's best known and most original personality" and Karl Johan Laurentius Torin, who had "a certain grandness of manner."[16]

Hagbard's years at *Skara läroverk* were successful. The examination results, June 5, 1895, showed good achievement in Christianity, Latin, Greek, French and German languages. His marks in history, geography, mathematics, physics and gymnastics were also quite good. He received marks of distinction (*med beröm godkänd*) in Swedish, Greek and music. When *Rektor* Julius Juhlin signed the original document authorizing Hagbard to enter the upper seventh Latin division he wrote: "Hagbard Brase has demonstrated good energy and his life is characterized by good conduct." The family was proud of Hagbard's progress. *Moster* Sofia (maternal aunt) wrote to him in June of that year: "I am writing to tell you dear boy that you have honored both yourself and your family. Your Uncle Ernst and I both congratulate you on your fine promotion."[17]

The former Skara student in later years looked back with great pleasure to the various activities in which he participated during school years. November 6 was Gustavus Adolphus Day. The traditional celebration included a torchlight procession and a program with patriotic speeches presented by the students. He recalled the feeling of those times: "To stand in *Krabbelund* (a small park) or *Botan* (the botanical garden) surrounded by flaming torches, singing or listening to the performance of *Begone, Oh Fleeting Memories of Time* (Viken tidens flyktiga minnen) made our hearts beat faster and tears came to our eyes."[18]

In the spring the whole school had a day off for what was called a

Skara läroverk pictured in 1900, where Hagbard Brase was a student until 1895.

"walking excursion" (*utmarsch*): "We walked by classes like a company of soldiers for six or seven miles to some famous place near Skara, perhaps to the ruins of a castle, or to an old country church, or to a place known for its natural beauty. We then enjoyed good food and fellowship." He also described another Skara tradition: "There was singing at *Krabbelund*, the park which was located near the school, or in *Botan*, the attractive botanical garden, every evening during the month of May. Romance was in the air. I was a part of this glorious life for several years. I have walked in these joyful processions on the cobblestones of the 'college' street between *Krabbelund* and *Botan* with good friends during happy years."[19]

The most festive time occurred in June at the end of a series of examinations which concluded the school experience. In April and May there had been written examinations to be followed in June by the oral examinations. The Minister of Education of the Swedish government appointed *censors* (examining commissioners) who participated with the teachers in the final oral examinations. When the formal activities were concluded, a large crowd of relatives and friends assembled outside the school to await the results.

Hagbard Brase has described this festive and dramatic occasion in considerable detail. At the appropriate moment the eyes of the spectators were focused upon a certain window in the main building of the school from which the custodian would make an announcement. Hagbard recalled one special occasion when the silence was broken and the word "*alla*" rang out loud and clear (all candidates had passed). Then Brase wrote: "Pandemonium broke out. Suddenly the big double doors opened and out came the new *studenterna* (qualified for entrance to a university) in their white caps, all in evening dress, as was the custom. As they came running, they had to pass between two rows of underclassmen who gave each one a terrific wallop on the back. At the end of the row they were met by parents, brothers, sisters, sweethearts and friends and loaded down with flowers. Then there were congratulations and 'hurrahs' for several minutes."[20]

The former Skara student recalled that following this first phase of the celebration, someone yelled, "Singers!" (*Sångare*). *Studenterna* then formed a procession two by two, preceded by the college male chorus singing the selection, *Sing About the Students Happy Days* ("Sjung om studentens lyckliga dar"). The destination was *Krabbelund*, the site for a ritual that Brase found hard to describe. Four to six boys would clasp hands, and facing each other, they tossed each of the new graduates in the air. This was done again and again. After ten minutes or so, the procession formed again and marched to *Botan* amidst much singing.[21]

When the procession arrived at *Botan*, there was another ceremony. A large number of boys, about fifty, stood close together in two lines facing each other and clasping hands. At one end, a new graduate was lifted up, lying with his stomach on the arms and hands of the human bridge, which, at the appropriate time, tossed him high into the air. When he came down he had moved a foot or two forward. He went up again and again until he came to the end of the row. This action was repeated with other graduates. When all was over at *Botan*, the procession returned to *Krabbelund* and the crowd dispersed gradually. A student ball in *Stadshotellet* (City Hotel) was featured the following evening. The events were concluded then to be resumed again next June when the members of another graduating class shared in these experiences.[22]

Although Hagbard Brase made good progress in the study of languages and other subjects, his interest in music continued to develop. He has described the situation as follows: "I sang in choruses and also bass in a quartet after my voice changed, or rather while it was changing. As a boy I had a good soprano voice if I would only 'sing out.' I taught myself how to play chorales on an old reed organ. One day I found a guitar in the attic belonging to my grandmother Jungner. I began to play it and wrote a guitar method. Nils Petersson and

Morbror Ernst Jungner.

Moster Sofia Jungner Linde.

LEFT: Interior of the Skara school auditorium.

RIGHT: Interior of the Skara cathedral.

I played duets that I composed. I also began to compose songs with piano accompaniment. *Morbror* (Uncle) Ernst was much impressed. When all this happened I do not really know. Perhaps I was 12 to 15 years old. I used to walk up and down my room singing anything that I could get hold of. My favorite was the *Toreador* song from *Carmen*. I showed some talent in drawing and received a prize once consisting of a book."[23]

Young Brase began to study music more seriously in 1895. His first teacher was Johan Fredrick Janson, the Skara cathedral organist and a music teacher at *Skara läroverk*. Hagbard has written: "I left the college in 1895 to spend all my time on music. I sometimes played for Janson at the cathedral and I always sang in the cathedral choir... Janson asked me how much I practiced: 'Two hours piano, two hours organ, two hours harmony each day,' I replied. 'That is not enough. You must practice all day,' he replied. I spent hours over Schmitt's five finger exercises, in fact until my fingers bled. Janson told *Morbror* Ernst that he could not keep up with me and that I was born with a knowledge of harmony." However, at this time, Hagbard's ambition was to become an architect. He spent much time drawing the elaborate church windows like the large one at Skara cathedral. He observed at this time: "Peculiarly enough I had no overwhelming desire to become a musician or anything else for that matter, but I evidently could work very hard."[24]

However, as Hagbard spent more time in practicing, playing and composing, and encouraged by those who were impressed with his musical talent, he decided that he would attempt to enroll in the Royal Music Academy (*Kongliga musikaliska akademien*), in the division known as the Royal Conservatory of Music (*Kongliga musikaliska akademien*). In 1880 this division had been given independent status for teaching and promoting music.[25]

In the autumn of 1896 Hagbard Brase passed the examination for entrance into the Royal Conservatory of Music in Stockholm. Since there was a long waiting list, he was not able to matriculate until January 1897, when he was one of five successful applicants from a list of twenty-five. He studied at Stockholm from January 1897 until June 1900.[26]

II.

Music Studies in Stockholm

The decision to study at the Royal Conservatory in Stockholm introduced Hagbard Brase to a world quite different from that which he had known previously. He has written "My first trip to Stockholm was memorable for me." There was great excitement as he approached the Swedish capital city for the first time. The train entered a tunnel while still out in the country as it proceeded via South Stockholm, which lies on a higher level than the rest of the city, and when it came out after several minutes, it crossed a low bridge over the outlet of Lake Mälaren. The passengers soon found themselves in *Gamla Stan* (Old Town) as the train rushed on. It was night and the effect was overwhelming. There were ships, various other sea-going craft and ferries with lights everywhere. The train moved on until it crossed the northern arm of Lake Mälaren after which it stopped at the Central Station.[1]

After spending the night at KFUM (like a YMCA), he went to the Royal Conservatory of Music, (*Kungl. musikaliska konservatorium*), Nybrokajen 11, with its imposing looking building and its well-arranged facilities. In the lobby young Brase found instructions for new students. He met by chance Arvid Andersson, a student, who assisted him with the arrangements for taking the entrance examinations in harmony, organ and piano. As indicated previously, his matriculation had been deferred until January 1897.

When Hagbard Brase came to Stockholm to begin his studies in early January 1897, he was somewhat familiar with the city. He lived for a short time on Götgatan in South Stockholm, where Karl Gustaf Lindblom, a second cousin, and he rented rooms in the same house. They moved about a year later to Bastugatan where they engaged

13

lodgings in the home of a kind and interesting elderly lady.

The objectives for Brase's study at Stockholm were clearly defined. He wished to become a fine musician and to qualify for diplomas and certification as an organist, music teacher and church singer, with top priority upon the first named purpose. His studies included organ, piano, voice, theory, church music, history of music and methods.

The teachers at the Royal Conservatory of Music were well-established in their profession and several of them were actively engaged in performing, composing and conducting. August Lagergren was Hagbard's principal organ teacher. A good performer, he was at that time organist in the chapel of the royal castle. Lagergren was a thorough teacher who had good knowledge of organ repertoire. A restless person, he walked around the large hall during lessons, stopping occasionally for a pinch of snuff. Brase recalled that he was very decisive about legato playing. The teacher used the book he had written, *Organ Method (Orgel-Skola)*, in his instruction. Brase has written about it: "I cannot understand how we organ students could play fluently and fast with the fingering he has indicated in his *Method*." A part of every lesson was devoted to improvisation. The improvisations were mostly built on choral themes. The Conservatory had an established organ repertoire which was required for graduation. Included were compositions by Bach, Mendelssohn, Lemmens, J. E. Eberlin, Rheinberger, Handel, A. Hesse, R. Schumann, J. G. Töpfer, Saint-Saëns, Theile, G. Mankell, H. Berens, M. Brosig, Buxtehude, C. Widor and N. Gade.[2]

The diploma in organ also required the achievement of established standards in piano performance and knowledge of repertoire. Brase's principal piano teacher was Oscar Bolander. His students, including Brase, felt that "Bolander's style was from the Mozart-Hummel school of piano playing." The teacher liked a neat "pearly" style. Prescribed compositions included works by Bach, Beethoven, Clementi, Kahlau, Reinecke, Rameau, Mendelssohn, Schubert, Raff, Scarlatti, and V. Lachner.[3]

Voice lessons were taught by Hjalmar Håkansson, who was also cantor in *Storkyrkan* (name of church). Hagbard sang regularly in this choir. On occasion he served as a substitute choir director for his teacher, and on one occasion at St. Maria Church, South Stockholm. Brase had voice lessons with Håkansson at the Conservatory and in the studio of the teacher's home. Håkansson had probably been a good singer, but Brase did not feel satisfied with him as a teacher. The repertoire required for certification as a church singer included compositions by Righini, Klein, Mendelssohn, Josephson, Lindner, Grell and Stenhammar.[4]

Theory was a vital aspect of Brase's studies at Stockholm. He shared in the talent and methods of two teachers, Aaron Bergenson and Conrad Nordqvist. The latter was also a conductor at the Royal Opera. Hagbard has described some of his assignments: "For Nordqvist I wrote a large number of accompaniments to folk songs. For a whole year I wrote a modulation and harmonization of a chorale each week. The modulation was really a short piano piece."[5]

In the spring of 1899, Brase was examined by the music faculty to determine if he was qualified for a diploma in organ. The examination lasted for several days. He was expected to play satisfactorily selected compositions from the repertoire listed above as well as to perform sight reading and improvisations. An *Andante* by Mozart was one of the selections for sight reading. The results of the examination were gratifying. The official grades (*betyg*), based on five terms of study, showed that Brase had "passed with distinction" (*med beröm godkänd*) in organ and piano performance, harmony and knowledge and care of the organ. Moreover, the official document affirmed that he was "a master in performance of chorales, transposition, modulation" and of the works of the sixteen composers of organ literature as listed previously.[6]

Hagbard Brase began his last year at the Royal Conservatory in the autumn of 1899. His objective was to earn diplomas as a music teacher and church singer. In addition to instruction in voice, piano, vocal and choral repertoire, he taught some boys the rudiments of music as partial preparation for teaching. Brase has described parts of this examination: "It was very hard. I sang a prepared song, a chorale unaccompanied with two verses, one of which was printed under the notes. I can still see myself standing alone in the middle of the big organ hall, trying to sing with good tone, correct pronunciation and breathing before an audience which must have been amused. At least I would have been amused if I had been a part of the audience. This was enough torture for one day." He had borrowed 100 songs from Stockholm publishers and thus he had taught himself to sing at sight fairly well.[7]

Other aspects of the voice examination have also been described by the young student: "One song given us to sing was in manuscript and the text was in Latin. I think Svedbom (Dr. Vilhelm Svedbom, a faculty member at that time and Director of the Royal Conservatory of Music 1901-15) was the composer. I was ushered into an empty room, handed the manuscript and left alone for a few minutes. I made a dash for the piano. It was locked. I looked at the text. Thanks to my studies at Skara I knew some Latin. There was a skip in the melody E flat-C sharp: it looked difficult. Then I was called into the room and sang." The examination also included, among other parts, questions on *Principles of Italian Singing (Italienska sångens grunder)* by Höijer-Vaccai, the Swedish version of Vaccai's well-known treatise.[8]

The results of these examinations constituted a tribute to the talent and effort of the student. The faculty of the Royal Conservatory stated on May 31, 1900, that on the basis of seven terms of study, Hagbard was certified as a music teacher. His grades were as follows: Vocal performance, satisfactory (*godkänd*); piano, with distinction (*med beröm godkänd*); and harmony, with special distinction (*berömlig*). He was also certified as a church singer after four terms of study with the grade of satisfactory (*godkänd*). The faculty statement also attested to his "general musicianship, voice production, ability to sing the Swedish Church chorales and knowledge of the liturgy."[9]

Young Brase greatly enjoyed the opportunity to hear good music in Stockholm. Conservatory students could attend without cost all concerts presented in the concert hall of that institution. This was one of the largest and finest concert halls in Stockholm. He heard many well-known pianists including Gabrilovitch, Bauer and Borowski and others as well as famous singers and instrumentalists. He was in the audience when Grieg presented a concert of his compositions. The great Norwegian composer accompanied some of his songs and conducted a large chorus. Brase enjoyed opera most of all. His favorite at the outset was *Cavalleria Rusticana* and *Pajazzo*; later he preferred *Carmen*, and towards the end of his stay in Stockholm, *Die Meistersinger* was his favorite. He was in attendance at the performances of Gounod's *Faust* and *Romeo and Juliet*, Mozart's *Don Juan*, *The Marriage of Figaro* and *The Magic Flute*, Wagner's *Lohengrin*, *Tannhäuser* and other great operas. Hagbard heard many oratorios, including two composed by Bach, *The Passion of Our Lord According to St. Matthew* and *St. John*; Brahm's *Requiem*; César Franck's *Salighetsstigar* (The Beatitudes); Dvorák's *Stabat Mater* and Handel's *Messiah*.[10]

Brase had several good friends in Stockholm. Almost all of them were associated with the Royal Conservatory. Among them were Arvid Andersson, Sigfried Nyrén, Martin Oscar and Adolf Wiklund. The latter was his closest friend. Wiklund later became a conductor at the Royal Opera. Oscar, a colorful young man, was a singer at the Royal Opera. In 1900 Hagbard and five other students organized The Academy's Student Society (*Akademiska förbundet*). He was chosen the first president. The organization was designed to include students in music and painting and others from the School of Technology. Their first formal activity was an evening social occasion (*Sexa*) when guests were invited. A dinner dance was held later. Hagbard recalled that he tried to dance but had to give up the attempt.[11]

Hagbard used his free time in a variety of activities. When he did not sing in a church choir, he attended church services at various congregations, often at Adolf Fredrik's church where Sjögren was organist or at St. Clara church, where Hägg had a similar assignment. On rare occasions he enjoyed Sunday dinner at a restaurant called Quiet Mary (*Tysta Mari*). He also visited *Skansen*, the famous outdoor museum, and *Djurgården*, looking at animals living in their natural habitat. Many Sunday afternoons were spent in the National Museum. Hagbard was invited occasionally to dine at the home of *Fröken* (unmarried lady) Warolin in the fashionable suburb of Djursholm. She financed a substantial part of Hagbard's last year at Stockholm. At *Fröken* Warolin's home he met Countess Taube, a daughter of the famous composer, Gunnar Wennerberg. Hagbard's father had been a tutor for the Wennerberg children.[12]

Hagbard joined the throngs of people who celebrated King Oscar's Twenty-fifth Jubilee and Exposition in 1897. This was a festive occasion. He saw the grand parade of the Royal family and foreign kings and princes as they rode in open carriages on the principal streets of Stockholm. In the evenings, brilliant fireworks were displayed at the harbor with magnificent illusions as the lights and colors were reflected in the water.

The Royal Conservatory of Music, Nybrokojvägen 11, in Stockholm, Sweden.

Hagbard was occasionally in great financial stress during the Stockholm years. Uncle Ernst and others provided loans but these funds were not sufficient. Whenever his mother could send five *kronor* (crown, currency unit) or even less, he was the grateful recipient. Food was sent to him, including molasses bread (*sirapsbröd*). His mother was worried that he might go to bed without having eaten enough. In 1898, when Hagbard was quite ill, she wrote: "I feel so badly for you, dear son... Be very careful about your food and clothing and do not over-exert yourself. Buy yourself a good bottle of Marsala (wine), since that is the best I know for the stomach. Oh, if you were only here so that we could take care of you. Do not forget that the most important of all is the prayer of your sad mamma." Hagbard wrote in his "Memoirs" that he lived occasionally on twelve *öre* (a few cents) per day for a cup of coffee and French bread.[13]

The son shared with his mother a report of several activities while at Stockholm and she responded in a variety of ways. When he told her about the novels which he was reading, she replied that she was "sad" and expressed the hope that he would not spend too much time reading that kind of literature. She did not criticize his attendance at the theatre and other entertainment which was available without cost to Conservatory students. However, she suggested that these activi-

Hagbard Brase.

Ingegerd Brase, Hagbard's sister.

ties should be described on a separate piece of paper so that Uncle
Ernst, who enjoyed reading Hagbard's letters, would not know about
this use of time by Hagbard. His mother was pleased with Hagbard's
description of the King's Jubilee in 1897, and in response to his description of the illumination of bridges and buildings in Stockholm,
she told him that at Skara there were candles and lamps in the windows of all the houses, that the schools and public buildings were il-
luminated and that choral groups sang on the streets to commemorate
the King's Jubilee. In 1898 Hagbard and his mother were delighted
that Ingegerd could spend a week with her brother in Stockholm, in
a joyous reunion.[14]

Other relatives also corresponded with Hagbard during his Stockholm years, including Brita Brase, his aunt, who lived in Bitterna.
She was proud of Hagbard's decision to study music at the Royal Conservatory but she expressed her hopes and prayers that "he would not
follow the call of temptation in the big city."[15]

When Hagbard completed his studies in Stockholm in June 1900,
he returned to Skara where he lived in *Moster* Sofia's home, Albano,
in the outskirts of the town. This was an old rambling house in good
condition, surrounded by a garden. When the Skara schools opened
in September, *Moster* Sofia's roomers, known as *Skultar*, arrived.
Hagbard then rented a room on Bommagatan next to the house in

Hagbard's first home on Bommagatan, Skara.

which he had lived when his mother, Ingegerd and he moved from Levene to Skara in 1884.[16]

Hagbard was now seeking a position as organist or music teacher. He was busy applying for positions in the few vacancies known to him. He earned his board and room by teaching music in Uncle Ernst's private school for elementary teachers.

However, something yet unknown to him was in the offing which would be decisive for the future. This development will be discussed following the description of an important personal event and an interesting interlude during the Stockholm years.

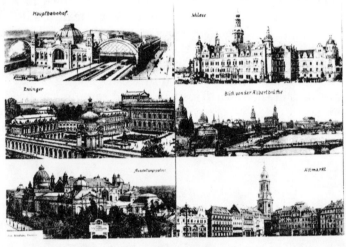

A postcard shows views from Dresden—one of the German cities visited by Hagbard Brase in the summer of 1899.

III.

An Interlude

In the summer of 1898 something happened that was destined to be written large in the life of Hagbard Brase. While spending this time in Skara, following the completion of his studies for that year at the Royal Conservatory, Hagbard met a young woman who was described by him as follows: "There was a girl in Skara that summer whose name was Minna Hernwall. She was seventeen years old. She stayed in Uncle Ernst's home. Her job was to do a little of everything in the household without being a hired girl. That means that she was a member of the family." Then he continued: "I remember her on one special occasion. Uncle Ernst had a summer home in Lundsbrunn, a summer resort near Skara. There was a family gathering in that place one afternoon or evening. She was there, of course, and I thought that she was sweet. I remember looking at her from behind some tall pines and vines."[1]

Minna, whose full name was Lydia Minna Maria Hernwall, the daughter of Gustaf Leopold Hernwall and Lydia Hilda Maria Håkanson, was born at Reftele, Småland. At the time Hagbard and she met at Skara, the Hernwall home was at Halmstad.[2]

A close friendship soon developed between seventeen year old Minna and twenty-one year old Hagbard. Their affection for one another developed steadily, and on December 27, 1898, they were informally engaged. The engagement was formalized in July 1899, when rings were exchanged at a festive dinner at the home of Minna's parents at Halmstad. Present in addition to Minna's parents were Gösta, her brother, and Ditten, her sister, and other relatives who lived in Halmstad. Notices of the engagement were sent to newspapers at Halmstad and Skara. Personal visiting cards announced the engagement to relatives and friends.[3]

There was a steady stream of correspondence between Hagbard and Minna in the interim of the two years before their marriage in a far-away place and under circumstances that could not have been anticipated at the time of their betrothal.

In June 1899 Hagbard accompanied *Rektor* (Principal, Head Master) Jungner, his uncle, as a traveling companion on a trip to Germany. It was sponsored by the Swedish Ministry of Education for a study of teaching methods in German schools. They left Skara on June 16, traveling through Göteborg, Halmstad, where Hagbard visited briefly with Minna at the railroad station, then to Trelleborg, from whence they embarked on a boat to Sussnitz and then by rail to Berlin. They stayed ten days at the Hotel Witt in Berlin.[4]

Berlin was interesting and offered many rewarding experiences to the Swedish travelers. Hagbard was thrilled by the performances of *Siegfried* and *The Marriage of Figaro* at the Opera House. Uncle Ernst and Hagbard attended church services where the latter was impressed with excellent choirs and organists. Visits to the famous *Thiergarten* and the *Botanical Garden*, where he learned that 30,000 different plants were growing, provided a variety of enlightening experiences. He liked the lively music at the outdoor beer garden. The museums provided great joy. He attended a learned lecture at Berlin University and he saw the colorful banners and caps of various student societies. He was impressed by the many monuments (*Denkmaler*) that had been created to commemorate outstanding persons in the history of the realm. Uncle Ernst had conferences with school officials. The Swedish visitors had considerable difficulty with the German language at the outset but Hagbard profited gradually from the seven years of German that he had studied at Skara.[5]

From Berlin the Swedish travelers made the trip to Dresden by train. Hagbard was delighted with the beautiful and historic city. His visit to the museum, Albertinum, was one of the great memories of the trip. The Michaelangelo collection left him almost speechless. He viewed with awe copies of the magnificient portrayal of *Day, Night, Evening* and *Morning*. The paintings in the *Gemaldegalerie*, especially Raphael's *Sistine Madonna*, were overwhelming. This experience was recounted by him as follows: "The room was full of people but there was a great quiet. In the other rooms there was some conversation, but here there was silence. Mary seemed to come as if from heaven with the Christ-child in her arms.... " The young Swede continued to be impressed: "As we stood there quietly, it seemed as if we all wanted Mary to step down from her exalted place. Think of the fantasy Raphael must have had, and the religious ecstasy he must have been in when he painted the Madonna." Hagbard viewed the Madonna on three occasions, once in the company of Uncle Ernst, who did not fully share his nephew's enthusiasm. Young Brase was also greatly inspired by Rembrandt's works. He spent much time in Dresden's museums and galleries.[6]

Hagbard attended concerts at Dresden, including a performance by Dresden's *Orpheus Chorus*. He greatly regretted that the opera season was over. He saw the statues of Wagner and Weber and the places where they had worked for so many years. He was enthusiastic in his description of the beauty of the Dresden Opera House. When he visited the Botanical Garden he was especially interested in the papyrus plants. The mountains known as "Saxon Switzerland" near Dresden provided beautiful scenery. While on an excursion, Brase saw the house in which Schiller lived when he completed *Don Carlos*.[7]

Hagbard was enthusiastic about the six-day visit in Lichtenstein, near the Bohemian border. Shortly after arriving there on July 12, a trip into the mountain terrain provided the most beautiful scenery that he had ever seen. Excursions into the countryside resulted in superlative comments. One day he walked on the route that Napoleon's army traveled when the futile attempt was made to conquer Russia in 1812. Hagbard stopped often to pick and eat delicious blueberries. Lichtenstein, a town of about 7,000 inhabitants, was idyllic in many respects. The young visitor was thrilled to view the mountains at sunset and to listen to the vesper bells at eventide.[8]

The two visitors had fine opportunities to learn about education in Lichtenstein. Uncle Ernst had several meetings with the *rektor* and faculty of the principal school. Hagbard visited music classes, choir rehearsals, other ensemble groups and private music lessons. His comments were generally favorable although he felt that the piano teacher interrupted too frequently with corrections so that the pupil lost feeling for the continuity of the composition. Some pupils played compositions by Bach and Beethoven with fine technique and interpretation. He enjoyed especially the rehearsals of the Lichtenstein Music Society. A piano was available each day for his use.[9]

Hagbard came to Leipzig on July 18 with keen anticipation and the reality even exceeded his expectations. He went first of all to St. Thomas' church where Bach had been cantor. He stood with great respect before the memorial statue raised in honor of the great composer by Mendelssohn at his own expense. He was thrilled as he walked on the streets that were so well known to Bach and he visited the places associated with his name. A prophetic spirit hovered over twenty-year old Brase as he entered St. Thomas' Church where Bach's *The Passion of Our Lord According to St. Matthew* was first performed on Good Friday 1729. The young Swedish visitor was destined to introduce and conduct this oratorio on the two-hundredth anniversary celebration of the *St. Matthew Passion* at Bethany College on Good Friday 1929. The streets in Leipzig named after great musicians—Beethoven, Mozart, Haydn, Schumann and others—witnessed to the cultural tradition of the city. At the Botanical Garden he enjoyed the music of Strauss conducted by the composer and played by an orchestra from Vienna.[10]

An excursion was made one day to Lützen. Here he was reminded of Lützen's role in history. The site of Sweden's King Gustavus Adolphus' death there in the Thirty Years War was dominated by a monument that was almost overwhelming in its size.

Wittenberg was the last city on the German itinerary. He visited the places associated with Martin Luther—the Reformer's room in the Augustinian monastery, the University where he lectured and the church with the door on which Luther was reputed to have nailed the ninety-five theses on the eve of the Reformation. Melanchthon's house, the City Hall and other historic sites enriched the visit to Wittenberg.[11]

Late in July Uncle Ernst and Hagbard began the return journey to Sweden. They stopped briefly at Lübeck, the old Hanseatic League city. At Travemunde, the Sound was like a mirror and there was not a cloud in the sky. A mass of bathers shouted to the travelers: "Have a pleasant trip!" When they boarded the ship, *Halland*, which was registered at Halmstad, Hagbard almost felt like throwing his arms around the neck of the stewardess as he heard Swedish spoken for the first time in several weeks. The schedule permitted only a brief stay at Copenhagen before crossing Öresund to Malmö in Sweden. Uncle Ernst and Hagbard parted company there; the former boarded a train for Nässjö, while the latter entrained for Halmstad. Upon his arrival there the formal announcement of his engagement to Minna Hernwall was made at a festive dinner occasion.[12]

The German journey was over. Hagbard unknowingly at this time was destined during the next year to make a much longer journey across the Atlantic Ocean to a small Swedish-American community in Central Kansas.

IV.

Emigration and Early Years in Lindsborg, 1900–1906

Hagbard Brase's future belonged not to Skara and Sweden but to Lindsborg and America. The latter community in Central Kansas had been founded in 1869 by Swedish immigrants under the leadership of Pastor Olof Olsson from Värmland. Slightly more than a decade later, in 1881, Bethany Academy was founded by Pastor Carl Swensson. This baccalaureate degree-granting Lutheran college of liberal arts and sciences emphasized music and art. Although the founder was a Swedish-American born in Pennsylvania, several of the faculty members were talented Swedish immigrants.

Included among the professors at Bethany College was Birger Sandzén, a graduate of *Skara läroverk* and a former student of Anders Zorn. In the summer of 1900 Sandzén wrote to his brother, *Komminister* Gustaf Sandzén, Närunga, Västergötland, stating that President Swensson of Bethany College was seeking a talented Swedish organist and music teacher for his faculty. Sandzén asked his brother to make inquiry if Hagbard Brase would be interested in the position. The former had read in a Swedish newspaper that Brase, who was known to him from boyhood years, had recently graduated from the Royal Conservatory. Gustaf Sandzén transmitted this inquiry to *Rektor* Ernst Jungner, Hagbard's uncle, who then informed his nephew about the position in Lindsborg.[1]

Young Brase was interested in knowing more about the opportunity of joining the Bethany faculty. There was an exchange of letters between Skara and Lindsborg. He discussed the possibility of going to America with Minna Hernwall, his fiancé, and with his family. In September a letter came from President Swensson inviting him to join the faculty of the college. In an autobiographical article published in

Morgontidningen, Göteborg, Hagbard Brase recalled the situation and his reponse to it: "When one is young one doesn't reflect long, and after two days I was ready for an answer. My principal adviser was the editor of one of Skara's newspapers, who had lived in America a few years. He advised me 'to look around and see the world' and not stay in America more than two years."[2]

Since the decision had been made, plans for the journey to America went forward immediately. Money was borrowed for travel expenses, tickets were purchased, baggage packed and farewells spoken. Göteborg was the port of embarkation for the first part of the journey. Hagbard was joined by sister Ingegerd and *Moster* Sofia from Skara and Minna and Ditten, her sister, from Halmstad. In the afternoon before the

LEFT: *Dr. Carl Aaron Swensson (1857–1904) was president of Bethany College at the time the invitation was made across the Atlantic to Dr. Brase, asking him to join the faculty of the College of Music and Fine Art at Bethany College. Swensson had been ordained in 1879 at age 22 as a Lutheran minister of the Augustana Lutheran Synod, and almost immediately he became pastor of Bethany Lutheran Church in Lindsborg, Kansas. In the sacristy of that church in 1881 he founded the academy that was to become Bethany College, and from the beginning he served as one of the instructors. Swensson was president of the College from 1889 until his death on February 14, 1904.*
RIGHT: *Sven Birger Sandzén, well-known artist, was on the Bethany College faculty full-time for 52 years, 1894–1946, plus eight more years as Artist in Residence and Professor Emeritus of Art until his death on June 14, 1954. He had known Hagbard Brase from boyhood years. Dr. Sandzén began the inquiries which led to Brase joining the Bethany faculty.*

sailing date, a coffee party for relatives and friends took place in the hotel where Hagbard stayed. In the evening members of the Brase party went to see a motion picture, the first one to be seen by Hagbard. He has pointed out that several years passed before he saw another one, at the open-air nickelodeon at Lindsborg.[3]

When Hagbard Brase left Göteborg enroute to England and then to the United States that October day in 1900, he began a journey that was destined to fashion decisively the rest of his life. Ingegerd, Minna and Uncle Almfelt (Hjalmar Almfelt), a friend of the family, who later married Ingegerd, were among those on the pier who wished him bon voyage.

The North Sea crossing to England was rough at times. The young traveler has written: "When I awakened the next morning in my cabin and began to dress, the mirror came towards me. I managed to get up on the deck and it went comparatively well the rest of the trip." The ticket for the passage from Göteborg to New York had been purchased from Sam Larsson for 225 Swedish kronor. The ship from Göteborg disembarked passengers at either Hull or Grimsby. The trip from the eastern coastal city was made by train. In London he only had time to send a postcard to Minna.[4]

Hagbard was among the 180 second class passengers who boarded the *S.S. New York* of the American Line which left Southhampton on October 20, 1900, for New York via Cherbourg. Young Brase soon became acquainted with a fellow passenger, a Swedish-Finnish portrait painter. He was friendly and helpful on the ship and at the New York customs inspection. Hagbard referred to him as his "guardian angel." The artist invited him to be his guest at his first meal in America and while he appreciated the invitation, he had difficulty with his initial attempt to eat oysters. When the two travelers reached Chicago, the artist invited Hagbard to be a guest in his home until the trip to Kansas began. At an evening social function at which Swedish was spoken by several people, Brase sensed that the conversation was full of politics. Everyone was a Republican and he was told that McKinley was certain to win the forthcoming presidential election.[5]

At Chicago Brase presented a letter of introduction from Dr. Carl Swensson, president of Bethany College, which enabled him to purchase a railroad ticket at a substantial discount. The trip from Chicago to Kansas City and then to Salina was uneventful. He boarded a Union Pacific train from Salina to Lindsborg, arriving there during the afternoon of October 30. Hagbard was met at the railroad station by Birger Sandzén. This was the beginning of an intimate, life-long friendship of the artist and the musician.[6]

Brase lived with Birger Sandzén in his newly built house on North

The Bethany College building which later became known as Old Main was built in the year 1886–87. It loomed large on the landscape of the Smoky Valley in central Kansas and in the minds of Bethany faculty, students, and friends. An imposing structure of five stories, it contained a chapel which could seat 850 persons, dormitory housing for 103 students, the library, recitation rooms, a museum and science areas, a large dining hall, and offices. The building was razed in 1968 when it no longer could be renovated for campus needs.

Second Street across from the Bethany campus until the latter's marriage with Frida Leksell in the early part of November. Hagbard then moved to the five-story main college building known so affectionately as Old Main by many generations of faculty and students. Living accommodations were in a northeast room on second floor. His studio was the northwest corner on the same floor. From it he could look across the broad Smoky Hill Valley, rimmed at the edge of the horizon by the Spanish Steppes, named to commemorate the visit of Francisco Vasquez Coronado and his conquistadors in 1541.[7]

Hagbard's first letter from Lindsborg to Minna Hernwall was dated November 2, 1900, two days after his arrival. It was written on an official Bethany College letterhead with elaborate photos of the institution's campus. In the letter he shared with Minna his first impressions of the community in which they were to make their home for more than half a century. A part of Hagbard's letter follows:

It appears that it will be very pleasant here. A few conditions are, it is true, a little strange but I believe that I will like it.... Everything is so quiet and peaceful but very enjoyable. The town is small. The streets are wide with small attractive houses on each side. Generally the Americans are more home centered in their lives than Europeans. There is no restaurant life. If one is unoccupied, one stays at home or visits with a friend. The air is so clean. Although Lindsborg is on the same latitude as Constantinople, this is not a southern climate. I sometimes feel almost as if I am in Sweden.... Birger Sandzén is so kind and friendly. It is so fine to have him here. He takes care of me.[8]

The newcomer was quite persuasive in his description of Lindsborg in this first letter:

Oh, if you knew how beautiful the weather is here The leaves have turned yellow and are beginning to fall, but there is no bad autumn weather. You are certain to like it here.... How happy, my dear, I would be if you were here with me. It is cheap to live in Lindsborg. Birger Sandzén says that a married couple can live on a small salary. Food is cheap here. Eggs, which you like so much, are 5 cents a dozen—5 cents is about 17 *ore*. One gets in purchases for $1.00 the equivalent of 3.60 *kronor* in Sweden. Birger says that furniture for a four room house can be purchased for less than $100. If it goes well for me, I hope that you will come next year.[9]

Hagbard discussed in the letter certain aspects of life which reflected the response in Lindsborg to the pioneer tradition and circumstances: "Rules of etiquette are not a matter of primary consideration; everything is to the highest degree free and easy; people are not pretentiously polite; they dress simply. At least that is what I have observed at this time." He also cited real assets: "Everything here is youthful and joyful, so that one has a good feeling about life." He was favorably impressed with Bethany College: the fine, well-constructed five-story main building, the large dormitory for ladies, the impressive music hall which he had been informed seated 3,000 people and the art building where Birger Sandzén taught painting.[10]

The newcomer was pleased with the twelve teachers who formed the faculty of the School of Music. He wrote to Minna: "There is much music here. Sunday evening I shall accompany the choir which will sing Gounod's *St. Cecilia Mass*. That will be my debut as an organist here." Brase, who had arrived in Lindsborg October 30, shared his music talent on an important public occasion less than a week after arrival in the community.[11]

Hagbard Brase thus began a career that continued for more than half a century until his death in March 1953. It was true as he has written: "I had moved suddenly from an old college town, Skara, and from a city like Stockholm, to a pioneer town on the prairies of Kansas." As indicated earlier in this chapter, Lindsborg was founded in 1869 when Pastor Olof Olsson, Sunnemo, Värmland, and approximately 100 Swedish immigrants settled in the Smoky Valley of Central Kansas. Bethany Lutheran church was founded in August of that year, a public school was soon established, a Swedish lending library was formed and a church choir was organized. Additional immigrants, members of an American born Swedish-American generation and non-Swedish settlers formed the population of Lindsborg which numbered 1279 in 1900, the year that Brase became a resident.[12]

A decisive development in the community's history had occurred in October 1881 when Pastor Carl Swensson founded Bethany Academy. At the time of Brase's arrival in the Smoky Valley, the institution had become a four-year college which had conferred baccalaureate degrees since 1891. In 1900 the organization of the institution provided for a College of Liberal Arts and Sciences, a College of Music and Fine Arts, a College of Business, an Art Department, a Normal Department (teacher education) and an Academy. More than 500 students enrolled during the academic year and thirty faculty members provided instruction.[13]

Music and art were emphasized early in the history of the college. Private lessons in voice and instruments and classes in music theory and history of music formed the basic music curriculum at the time of Brase's arrival. The college sponsored an oratorio society of 400 voices, a symphony orchestra, a chamber music ensemble, a band and smaller choral groups. Brase, who succeeded Hugo Bedinger, Swedish organist and teacher, who had resigned to become organist at Västerås cathedral in Sweden, joined a faculty of talented musicians which in-

The eight-sided Ling or "Messiah" auditorium had been built by the time Brase arrived in Lindsborg, and the excursion trains were becoming popular for travel to the Easter-week Messiah Festival oratorios and other musical events.

cluded Sigfried Laurin, Samuel Thorstenberg, Theodore Lindberg, Charles D. Wagstaff, George Hapgood and others. Later such esteemed musicians as Oscar Lofgren, Thure Jaderborg, Oscar Thorsen, Arvid Wallin, Hjalmar Wetterstrom and Leonard Gunnerson were colleagues.

Decisive in Hagbard Brase's early years at Bethany College was the impact of Dr. Carl Swensson, founder and president. His earthly pilgrimage came to an end in fewer than four years after Brase's arrival in Lindsborg. The young teacher remembered clearly in later years his first meeting with Swensson. What happened then was written in *The Lindsborg News*, November 9, 1900: "A hearty welcome was accorded Dr. Swensson last Saturday evening at the Union Pacific depot. The whole college family was there. The band played and all cheered when the doctor stepped down from the car." Swensson had returned to Lindsborg after a long campaign trip in behalf of the candidacy of William McKinley for president of the United States. Brase has recorded his remembrance of the occasion: "There was a big crowd at the station. Swensson walked towards me almost as soon as he stepped from the train and greeted me welcome as only he could do." Young Brase then and later had high esteem and respect for Dr. Swensson as he wrote: "These were busy days at Bethany. Many of the teachers were young and Swensson was the soul of the community. He made an indelible impression on me as well as on all who came under his influence."[14]

Brase's first year (1900-01) at Bethany College involved him in a full schedule of teaching, performing and composing. He taught thirty private lessons in organ and piano. Fifty-two students were enrolled in his Harmony classes. As already indicated, he was at the organ when the oratorio society presented Gounod's *St. Cecilia Mass*, shortly after his arrival in Lindsborg. Later in the autumn he played organ solos at a teachers' recital. During the "Messiah" Festival, March 31–April 7, 1901, he was organist at five performances of Handel's *Messiah*. In five faculty concerts during the week he opened each program with an organ solo on the three-manual Möller pipe organ. Prior to

Excursion trains for the Messiah Festival, on the tracks east of Ling or "Messiah" auditorium.

the festival there had been a series of twice weekly rehearsals and much time was spent in practicing organ and piano. As will be described later, it was during this period that he was heavily involved in composing seventy selections published as *Körsånger* (choir songs) in 1901.[15]

Although Hagbard Brase was fully engaged in the life and work of the college during his first year, his thoughts were often turned toward Minna in faraway Halmstad. His feeling for her now that he lived in America was quite likely even more deep-seated than when he had written to her from Germany during his trip there with Uncle Ernst. At that time he shared the following with Minna: "I have *hemlängtan* (longing for home) as one says, tonight. Uncle is very lucky since he has his own home. You cannot sense what it means to be homeless. Minna, it would be so fine if you could leave your parents' home and we could have our own little home. Let us hope that it will not be only in the far too distant future. That I do not believe. In any event, we are both young. Well, the longer one waits, then so much

The chapel in old main was a beautiful, functional facility when it was built in 1886—fourteen years before Brase arrived in October of 1900.

more beautiful will it be when it occurs. That is, if one does not wait too long."[16]

As Brase had reflected on the situation while in Germany in 1899, he had thought about Ingegerd, his sister: "May Inga [Ingegerd] also have her own home soon because she will find it more difficult than I to be homeless. I have both of you and she has only me, and I am not as good a brother as I should be and for that I will be regretful some day. This last year must have been terribly difficult for her." (Their mother died in 1898.) Hagbard then expressed the hope that Minna and his sister would be close friends. In that context he wrote the following: "Ingegerd said that evening when I told her we were engaged, 'She is the dearest sister-in-law that I could have.' "[17]

Hagbard, in Lindsborg, far away from Minna in Halmstad, has described their response to the separation: "I was writing numerous letters to Minna, telling her how easy it was to establish a home in America, which was true enough, and how cheaply people could live here. From my letter to her it seemed as if I had to convince her. This she denies emphatically." Minna shared the loneliness of separation from Hagbard. As the correspondence developed, the mutuality of the desire to be together intensified. The decision was made—Minna would join Hagbard in Lindsborg. When Miss Amelia Rabenius, a member of the Bethany faculty and resident head of the ladies' dormitory, returned to Lindsborg in September 1901, following a visit in Sweden, she was accompanied by Minna Hernwall.[18]

A joyous meeting occurred between Hagbard and Minna on September 21, 1901. The former has described this memorable occasion: "I met them in Salina with a horse and buggy. A student was the driver. We were married by Dr. Swensson that evening in the Sandzéns' home. After the ceremony the Sandzéns had a wedding supper for us. Those present were Dr. and Mrs. Swensson, Mr. and Mrs. Erik Leksell, Miss Rabenius, Oscar Thorsen, the Sandzéns, Minna and I." A male quartet and a female quartet sang at the wedding. Mrs. Sandzén had intended to serve some homemade wine but it had disappeared. A member of the girls' quartet told the Brases twenty-five years later that the boys in the quartet helped themselves to the wine which they found on the kitchen porch.[19]

The Brase's first home was a rented small house on the west side of Second Street near the Bethany campus, south of their later and final residence. There were only two rooms and a hall. A few months later they rented a larger, one-story house on the same street near the southwest corner of the campus.[20]

Students and other visitors to Hagbard's studio at the college saw what he described as "Minna's wonderful photo" on the table. It was

A wedding photograph of Hagbard and Minna Brase. The couple had first met in the summer of 1898 in Sweden, and trans-Atlantic correspondence continued after Brase emigrated to America. Minna Hernwall agreed to join Hagbard Brase in Lindsborg, and they were married in the home of Birger and Frida Sandzén on September 21, 1901— the same day Minna first stepped foot in Lindsborg.

undoubtedly true as he stated that "Minna was a great sensation when she came to Lindsborg." She was a beautiful woman who retained her distinctive beauty with the passing of the years. Her husband thought that "she looked like a queen." Minna was more fashionably dressed than the young women at the college and in Lindsborg at that time. Hagbard also observed that "Since Minna knew no English at that time, she may have seemed more retiring than she actually was."[21]

The newly married couple had the great resources of mutual love and esteem. Understandably there would be difficult problems of adjustment to American life. Young and talented, they faced the challenge of the unknown future. They accepted the challenge, and what they achieved was good and meaningful.

The Brases began their life together during a year of celebration at Bethany College. Only six weeks had passed since their marriage when they became active participants in the celebration of the twentieth anniversary of the founding of the college. They were a part of the large crowd who welcomed Bishop and Mrs. K. H. G. von Scheele of Visby, Sweden, at the Lindsborg Union Pacific railroad station and joined in the procession led by the band as the distinguished visitors rode in a carriage down Main Street to the home of Dr. and Mrs. Swensson. The next three days were packed with events. On Sunday morning Bishop von Scheele preached an outstanding sermon. Brase presided at the organ for the prelude and hymns. In the afternoon the Brases were in the audience when speakers in Swedish, English, French, German, Latin, Greek and Hebrew saluted the college in seven of the fourteen presentations. At the evening program in the college auditorium, Brase's name appeared often on the program. He had composed the music for the *Cantata*, written in Swedish by *Kyrkoherde* J. P. Sandzén, father of Birger Sandzén; he had composed the *Gustava Festival March*, dedicated to the Bishop's wife, and played it on the organ; he was the organist when the oratorio society sang three choruses from *Messiah*.[22]

The anniversary celebration continued the next day with such varied events as a lecture by Bishop von Scheele on the subject, "The Development of Christianity," and a football game between Cooper College [Sterling College] and Bethany. In the evening Mrs. Brase saw her first American torchlight parade by students. The procession moved from the college through the residential district to Main Street "with torch lights, banners,transparencies, a constant display of Roman candles producing a rain of fire. College and class yells rent the air. At 9:00 p.m.the banquet started at the college dining hall; it lasted until Tuesday morning." The editor of *The Lindsborg News* wrote: "Everyone was happy and cheerful. It was a delightful event."[23]

The anniversary celebration closed on Tuesday, November 12, with a festive program in the auditorium. A special Bethany Choir performed a cantata with text by the Reverend Mauritz Stolpe and music by Hagbard Brase. The Bishop presented a lecture, "Christianity and Culture," which was described in *The Lindsborg News* as "masterly, scholarly and profound." At the end of the program the Bishop announced that King Oscar II of Sweden had designated President Carl Swensson as a commander of the Royal Order of the North Star. The entire audience arose and remained standing when the Bishop presented the insignia of the order to Dr. Swensson.[24]

Three years later the Brases shared with Bethany College, the Lindsborg community and people in a wide area the grief caused by the unexpected death of Dr. Swensson at the age of forty-nine on February 14, 1904, at Los Angeles. On a farm near Lindsborg, Mrs. John Holmquist wrote in her diary, enclosed in wide black lines, a few words which expressed the sentiments of the people in the Smoky Valley: "I can scarcely see to write tonight on account of tears since we have received the news that Dr. Swensson is dead....It seems so strange that one who was so needed should have been taken away from his place of service."[25]

Hagbard Brase grieved as did many others to lose a friend, colleague and leader at the height of his great career. Swensson had initiated the contacts that brought Brase to Lindsborg. The young teacher's relationships with Carl Swensson had been pleasant and rewarding. February 22, 1904, the day of the memorial service, was bright and clear—"a Carl Swensson Day" people called it. When 3,000 people filled the auditorium beyond normal capacity, Brase played appropriate organ selections as the people walked slowly past the bier of the beloved Carl Swensson. Later he accompanied the oratorio society as organist during the singing of "Worthy Is The Lamb" from Handel's *Messiah*.

Although Brase was heavily involved as organist with the oratorio society, which annually presented four or five performances of *Messiah* and in solo organ appearances, he was also occupied with other activities. He has described his situation as follows: "How I worked during those years, not only teaching private pupils and classes and practicing a great deal, but I also learned the English music vocabulary. I worked a great deal on theory courses which had been neglected. All my spare time was given to composing."[26]

The young teacher soon enriched the curriculum in music theory. When he joined the faculty in 1900, there were two courses: harmony and counterpoint. Three years later the schedule of courses included harmony, counterpoint, musical form and analysis, double counterpoint, canon and fugue and instrumentation. Shortly thereafter the enrollment grew substantially with more than eighty students enrolled in the theory classes.[27]

The courses in organ were also enriched in 1902-03 and in the reorganization, four divisions were provided: 1. Preparatory 2. Intermediate 3. Certificate 4. Organist diploma course. Each division presented specific studies ranging from pedal exercises, chorales, preludes and service playing, with progressive repertoire in the Intermediate and Teacher's Certificate courses, to be consummated by the Organist Diploma, which included among the following: greater Preludes and Fugues by Bach, Sonatas by Mendelssohn, Rheinberger and Guilmant; selected movements from symphonies by Widor; compositions by Buxtehude, Theile, Saint-Saëns, Franck and other classical and modern compositions. Although the enrollment was not large, there was a goodly number of fine students.[28]

Brase, as indicated above, stated that "All my spare time was given to composing." This commitment received special emphasis shortly after the young teacher's arrival as recorded in his "Memoirs": "Through the influence of Dr. Swensson I was commissioned by the Augustana Book Concern, Rock Island, Illinois, to compose an anthem for each Sunday and special days in the church year. I also wrote the text for the compositions from the selected gospel for the day according to the pericope of the Lutheran Church."[29]

The Bethany composer's choir anthems were published by the Augustana Book Concern in four separate volumes and later combined into a single volume with the title *Choir Songs for Soprano, Alto, Tenor and Bass with Texts from the First Series of Gospels (Körsånger För Soprano, Alt, Tenor och Bas med Text ur förste årgångens evangelier)*. The first volume, which covered the period from the First Sunday in Advent to the Fifth Sunday After Trinity, was published in the early autumn of 1901. The other three sections and the complete volume were published during the following year.[30]

Hagbard Brase, with customary modesty, deprecated his *Körsånger*: "The style of my ill-fated *Körsånger* was too difficult for choirs and congregations brought up, for instance, on *Hemlandsånger*, a popular hymnal with favorite evangelical hymns." He declared that his compositions "show an inexperienced hand." Although there was not a good response in sales, Brase's anthems received praise from the Reverend Alfred Ostrum, who reviewed them in *Augustana*: "The music is churchly, of high quality, beautiful and inspiring.... Choir members who have some experience in singing and a taste for high quality church music will not find these songs difficult but immensely interesting in sustaining enthusiasm and eagerness to elevate choir singing. We heartily thank Professor Brase for these excellent *Körsånger* and we hope that his noble undertaking will be so generally appreciated that he will feel encouraged to present us with additional proof of his rich harmonious creativity."[31]

Although Hagbard Brase was successful and well-liked at the college and Minna and he were adjusting quite well to American life, there were problems and uncertainty about the future. Hagbard, while reflecting on these early years, wrote later: "Our hearts should have been 'young and gay' but I do not think that they were. Our thoughts and feelings were in Sweden. We had few acquaintances; our only friends were the Sandzéns. We were desperately poor. My salary was about $600 a year, which was paid irregularly, and sometimes not at all. All our furniture and most of our kitchen utensils were bought on credit. In addition, I had debts in Sweden. With the help of Uncle Ernst and others I had been able to borrow money I needed for my studies in Stockholm. This must now be paid back. Several times I sent money to *Moster* Sofia, who then paid on a bank loan I had in Skara. It took several years before I had cleared this debt." The financial situation was always a problem because of the low salaries at the college.[32]

In 1905 Hagbard and Minna, already blessed with an active and darling daughter, Thorborg, born August 9, 1902, discussed plans for the future. He has described the situation: "In the early spring of 1905 we had some difficult problems to solve. We expected our second child to be born in June. Minna could not take care of the children and the house alone. No help was available. Other families in similar circumstances had relatives or close friends. As a last resort Minna decided to go back to her parental home in Sweden. Dr. Arvid Pihlblad, our physician, whom we consulted, thought that the trip would be good for her. Minna left for Sweden in the company of Miss Rabenius. Hagbard received in August the good news from Halmstad that a daughter, Karin Ingegerd, had been born on July 30, 1905."[33]

When Minna and Thorborg left for Sweden, Hagbard arranged for the storage of their furniture in the parsonage of the Bethany Lutheran Church and moved to a room in Professor Ekholm's house. Samuel Holmberg, a talented young painter and an art teacher at the college, lived there also. Brase and other teachers prepared their meals in the college dining hall during the summer months. One of their colleagues, Adolph J. Friedman, arranged for barrels of beer to be available from time to time in closets on second and third floors of the main building. Hagbard remembered later the hard work required to roll the heavy beer barrels up the steep stairs.[34]

The academic year 1905-06, when Minna and their two daughters

The faculty of the College of Music and Fine Art at Bethany College is pictured in Forget-Me-Not Annual, 1902, published by Bethany College. Dr. Carl A. Swensson is in the center. Among those in the third row are Dr. Brase (fourth from left), his close friend Dr. Birger Sandzen (fifth from left), and Prof. Thure Jaderborg (sixth from the left).

were in Sweden, was not a pleasant time for the husband and father. He has described the situation: "All my spare time was given to com posing. Laurin [Sigfried Laurin], Professor of Piano, played a *Ballad in F Minor* which I composed. It was very difficult but I believe that he liked it. I composed a group of piano numbers which were called *Sunflowers*." Although Brase's classes and lessons went well, he was lonesome for his family. His feelings were expressed as follows: "This was the longest year of my life."[35]

The current situation merged with a more permanent factor in the life of the Brases. Hagbard has explained the background in these words: "During these years Minna and I had always dreamed about the time when we could return to Sweden. That time seemed to have come. Minna and our children, Thorborg and Karin, were already there. In the spring of 1906 I made preparations for going to Sweden, and if possible, to remain there. I even had such ambitious thoughts as studying composition in Germany." Hagbard had decided that he would join his family in the land of his birth.[36]

Hagbard Brase, circa 1901.

V.

To Sweden and Lindsborg Again

In May 1906, after the end of the academic year, Hagbard Brase enthusiastically prepared for the trip to Sweden and the opportunity to join his family after a year's separation. In the company of Joseph Fogelberg, teacher of Swedish and Latin at Bethany, he traveled by train to New York. He borrowed money from his insurance company there, ordered a new suit of clothes and did some sightseeing. When he was asked for identification papers at the insurance office, he had difficulty in producing such evidence. However, when he had occasion to use a handkerchief with "H.B." embroidered thereon, the problem of identification was solved. Hagbard spent happy days at New Haven, Connecticut, where he visited Bethany College graduates who were enrolled in the Yale Graduate School. In 1902, *The Yale Alumni Weekly* had stated that "There are more graduates of Bethany College at the Yale Graduate School than from any other college, Yale excepted." This fine Bethany Yale tradition prevailed at the time of Brase's visit there.[1]

The Atlantic crossing was made in early June 1906 from New York to Glasgow on the *S.S. Caledonia* of the Anchor Line. One of the passengers was Swedish-born Gustavus Adolphus Peterson, a graduate of Gustavus Adolphus College, St. Peter, Minnesota, and a Master's degree recipient from the University of Minnesota, who was enroute to Europe for language study in Germany. A close friendship was to develop between Brase and Peterson when the latter joined the Bethany faculty in 1907. In Scotland Brase visited Edinburgh, where he was interested in the Palace of Holyrood House, Maria Stuart's room, Knox House, and other historic places.[2]

41

Embarking from Grimsby, Hagbard crossed the North Sea to Göteborg, and then he traveled by rail to Skara where he arrived about Midsummer Day 1906. It was a happy meeting for Minna and Hagbard after a year's separation. They went immediately to *Moster* Sofia Linde's home where Minna and the children were staying. There Hagbard saw Karin for the first time, "dressed in some white fluffy things." The happy father wrote: "I was almost overwhelmed when I first saw Karin. She was not yet a year old. She was so sweet that I thought I had never seen anyone like her."[3]

The Brases had an interesting and delightful summer in Sweden. The first two weeks were spent in Skara. There Hagbard visited *Skara läroverk*, the cathedral and other historic places. He relived in memory that time when at the age of ten he enrolled in the college. He leisurely visited *Krabbelund* and *Botan* and other areas that had meant so much to him in youthful years. A large part of the visit in Västergötland took place at Lundsbrunn, a summer resort ten miles from Skara, where Uncle Ernst had a summer home. Some visitors "took the baths" for which Lundsbrunn was famous and others "drank the waters." Ingegerd, Hagbard's sister, and Valborg Jungner, a cousin, were also at Lundsbrunn for a few days.[4]

Several excursions were made in the Skara area. One day was spent at Count Sparre's estate. Considerable time was devoted to Kinnekulle, one of Sweden's most beautiful mountains, located directly north of Skara near Lake Vänern. Läckö Castle, which traced its origin to the fourteenth century, was the destination for one delightful excursion. The visit to Råda, Hagbard's birthplace, was memorable. Minna and he stood silently and thoughtfully at the graves of his parents. They viewed the many thriving trees that his father had planted many years ago in the area. Hagbard played the old organ in the church. The keyboard was very old; the keys, normally white, were black, as was the pattern a hundred or more years ago. In late summer they were at Levene, the birth-place of Hagbard's mother and his residence as a boy during four years. They were guests of Hagbard's uncle, *Komminister* David Oskar Jungner and his family. Grandfather Johan Jungner had been *kyrkoherde* there. They also saw the graves of his maternal grandparents at Levene.[5]

While in Skara in July, Hagbard had a good visit with Birger Sandzén and Oscar Thorsen, natives of Västergötland and colleagues at Bethany College. The Sandzéns were visiting relatives and friends in Sweden. Thorsen had the same mission while enroute to Berlin where he later studied piano with Ansorge and Scharwenka. This was a happy day as the three friends leisurely walked around Skara, drank coffee out-of-doors and talked about Sweden and America. The only friend whom Hagbard met in Sweden that summer from his years at Stockholm was Arthur Wiklund.[6]

The summer months passed rapidly into early autumn as the Brases contemplated the future. It was becoming apparent that the hope of finding a permanent music position and residence in Sweden would not be realized. It was estimated that there might be a long delay since the prospects of finding an organist's position or a teaching post seemed to be discouraging. Moreover, his talent and services were needed at Bethany College where his former position was still available. Friends in Lindsborg urged the Brases to return to Kansas.[7]

When the decision had been made to leave Sweden, Minna and the children spent the last weeks in Halmstad with relatives. Hagbard was a welcome guest at *Moster* Sofia's home in Skara. These were days of sadness. There seemed to be something so bleak about the future which did not include permanent residence in Sweden. He visited for the last time *Skara läroverk* and the cathedral; he said sad farewells to relatives and friends. He then joined Minna and the two children for the last week in Sweden. Hagbard wrote with deep feeling about this farewell to the land of his birth: "It was very hard for us to leave Sweden this time. When the ship left Göteborg for England, we stood on the deck until the last cliffs and cobbles in the scurry disappeared behind the horizon." The Brases boarded the *S.S. Republic* of the White Star Line at Liverpool on September 28, 1906, for the Atlantic crossing to Boston. They were four of the ninety-four passengers in the second class. Agda Fred, Skara, accompanied them and helped Minna in caring for Thorborg and Karin. The ocean voyage was pleasant. At a concert on the ship, Hagbard played a piano solo as the opening number of an extensive music program. The long rail journey from Boston to Lindsborg required three days.[8]

On October 12, *The Lindsborg Record* reported the following: "Professor Brase [and his family] returned from the trip to Sweden Wednesday night on the flyer and is now ready to take up his work at the college. His many friends are glad to see him back again."[9]

Hagbard Brase had written from Sweden to his good friend, G. N. Malm, requesting his assistance in finding housing for the family. The only residence available was a small frame house with two rooms on the east side of Second Street near the college campus. The stored furniture was moved into these cramped quarters. A few months later Hagbard observed that a house was being moved to a vacant lot on the other side of the street from their present residence. He rushed over to make inquiry about rental from Mr. Almquist, the owner of the property. Arrangements were made then and there. Soon the Brases moved into more comfortable quarters.[10]

*Minna Brase and
daughters Thorborg
and Karin.*

The newly returned family now faced problems of adjustment to life in America. Minna for more than a year, and Hagbard for several months, had enjoyed a delightful way of living among relatives and old friends in familiar places. It is also to be remembered that their plan to take up permanent residence in the old homeland had not been possible.

An honest appraisal of their situation is found in Hagbard's "Memoirs": "We now had to become accustomed to Lindsborg once again. I remember how cramped our lives seemed to be. We lived in the north end of town. A mile south was the mill. That was all. For several months we had not heard any small town gossip or college and church politics. We were not in harmony with our surroundings. Minna especially could not overcome her longing for Sweden for many years. Has she ever been reconciled to live here all her life?"[11]

This intimate longing for the company of relatives and friends as well as for familiar places and experiences in the land of birth has been a normal and trying aspect of the lives of immigrants from all countries. While longing for home was always a present reality and filled the temple of memory with supportive resources, the Brases made

Prof. Oscar Thorsen.

Prof. Oscar Lofgren (standing), Prof. Sigfried Laurin.

the transition quite satisfactorily. They entered fully into the life of the community and rejoiced in the happiness which came to them through their growing family.

Hagbard Brase's contribution to the college increased steadily through teaching and performing. The number of organ students increased so that in the academic year 1909-10 there were twenty-six private students, who had one or two lessons per week. Moreover, the curriculum of the college had been enriched so that students could attain the bachelor of music degree with a major in organ. The theory program was also developed with more courses. Enrollment approached 100 students in two or three hour classes each term.[12]

Brase was also deeply involved as organist for the oratorio society, which was gaining in quality of performance and reputation. As indicated earlier, he served as organist for the first time in the 32nd performance of *Messiah* in 1901. When he was appointed director in 1915, he had been organist for fifty-eight renditions. In the early years *Messiah* was sung on five occasions during the annual Music Festival. These performances were preceded by semi-weekly rehearsals in which Brase had responsibilities. In addition, during his years as organist, the chorus presented seventeen other oratorio performances: Haydn, *Creation*, 5; Mendelssohn, *Elijah*, 4; Dvorak, *Stabat Mater*, 3; Cherubini, *Requiem Mass in C Minor*, 2; and one performance each of Gounod, *Mass Solennelle*, Mendelssohn, *Hymn of Praise* and Bach, *Christmas Oratorio*. He also performed on the organ at faculty recitals during Festival Week and on other occasions.

The lack of time impaired seriously Brase's opportunity for composing, a situation that he often lamented. However, in 1910, the Augustana Book Concern published his *Selected Chorales in Old Rhythmic Form (Valda Koraler i gammalrytmisk form)* consisting of twelve compositions for congregational singing. He presented them with the hope that "they might in some measure create interest in and love for the old Lutheran tradition of congregational singing and help to promote reform in church singing even within the Swedish Lutheran church in America."[13]

Included among the other music activities of Brase in this period were concerts dedicating new organs in churches at Norman, Oklahoma; Holdredge, Nebraska; Independence, Ellsworth, Mariahdal church near Cleburne, Kackley, Lindsborg, Kansas; and others. He was also conductor of the Bethany Male Chorus for a brief period.

Life for the Brases and others in Lindsborg was greatly enriched through a series of annual celebrity concerts by well known artists. Lillian Nordica sang to a packed auditorium in 1902 and again in 1904. On both occasions her singing was acknowledged by "thunderous applause." Other artists who appeared in Lindsborg during this period were Johanna Gadski, 1906; Jennie Norelli, 1912; Schumann-Heinck, 1913; Alice Nielsen and Eugene Ysaye, 1914. The Boston Symphony Orchestra in 1903-04, and the Innes Band in 1905 and 1907, performed at the college. Brase, who contributed directly to the cultural life of the college and community, shared with his colleagues in promoting these concerts.

Although the Brases were immersed in the American scene, they were not completely cut off from the tradition of the old country. In the early years Swedish was the common language in conversation, in the worship services and often in business relationships and public functions. The Swedish weekly newspaper, *Lindsborgs-Posten*, was published 1898-1930. It included local news, church notices and extensive space devoted to news from Sweden. For Lutherans, *Augustana*, a weekly Swedish journal, an official publication of the Augustana Synod, had many subscribers in the Smoky Valley. Hagbard Brase contributed articles about church music to this journal. Moreover, Birger Sandzén, Oscar Thorsen, G. A. Peterson and many other friends were Swedish-born.

There were several Swedish societies at Bethany College. Numbered among them were *Svea Vitterhets Sällskap* (Svea Literary Society) and *Tegnér Förbundet* (Tegnér Society), named after Esaias Tegnér, famous poet. It was not until 1923 that students of Swedish parents were excused from studying the Swedish language. The Bethany College colors, yellow and blue, were those of the Swedish flag. Bethany athletic teams were urged on to victory by the official college yell, *"Rockar Stockar, Thor och Hans Bockar"* in which Thor, the Nordic god, was called upon to aid the football team in driving through the line for a touchdown.

Special events at the college were often related to the Swedish background. In May 1907 there was a festive program in the college auditorium as one phase of the bicentennial observation of the birth of Carl von Linné, internationally known Swedish botanist. In January 1908 a memorial service following the death of King Oscar II the previous month was held with Birger Sandzén as the principal speaker. The college and community observed a series of Swedish festivals. In the latter part of April, *Valborgsmässoafton* (Walpurgis Eve celebration) was observed. This event was described in the *Bethany Messenger* as a student festival designed "to send into inglorious exile all the evil spirits that might have accumulated during the year" and in which "merriment, song and a good bonfire are the three requisites." *Julotta* (Christmas Matins) always brought a large congregation of worshippers at 5:00 a.m. to celebrate the birth of the Christchild.[14]

The Brase children: Thorborg, Yngve, and Karin.

Lindsborg entertained many Swedish and Swedish-American journalists. Jakob Bongren, John Enander, Anders Schön and Ernst Skarstedt were among the latter who came to visit and write about life in the Swedish community in Central Kansas. Well-known journalists and authors from Sweden also included Lindsborg on their itinerary. In 1902 Carl Sundbeck, author of the volume, *Svensk-Amerikanerna* (*The Swedish Americans*) met members of the faculty at a reception in the home of Dr. and Mrs. Swensson. He was impressed by the high level conversation in English and Swedish and by the fact that Swedish was generally used on Main Street. He was pleased to observe that he found copies of Swedish classics in the bookstore. G. D. H. von Koch, a journalist with *Svenska Dagbladet*, Stockholm, and author of *Emigranternas Land*, 1910, (*The Land of the Immigrants*), visited in 1910. He found that Swedish was still used widely in Lindsborg. He felt, however, that the community was on the threshold of a transition that would result soon in greater Americanization.

The evidence is quite complete that Hagbard and Minna Brase and other people of Swedish ancestry were not completely in an alien milieu. The language and customs of the old country were still viable at the beginning of the second decade of the twentieth century. Change was in the air. The Brases became a part of that change, and in that transition they had the cultural resources of the Old and the New

Worlds to challenge and to stimulate their lives.

A vital factor in the transition was the influence of their growing family. Thorborg, born in Lindsborg in August 1902, and Karin whose birth occurred in Sweden in July 1905, were joined in February 1909 by Yngve, the only son. Swedish was the mother tongue of the older children. The Brase children soon became involved with other children, Swedish-American and others, in a variety of personal contacts and activities. This development brought new interests and friendships. Life was busy and challenging.

In the fifteenth year of Hagbard Brase's tenure as a faculty member, a development took place that became paramount in his life and career and in the history of the college and community. After having established excellent credentials as an organist for the Bethany College Oratorio Society for a decade and a half and as a fine musician, Hagbard Brase was the logical choice to be the director of the oratorio society when a vacancy occurred. He was selected for that important position with the oratorio season in the "Messiah" Festival of 1915. The next chapter is devoted to his distinguished career as director of the Bethany College Oratorio Society for somewhat more than three decades.

Hagbard and Minna Brase were among those who greeted Bishop and Mrs. K. H. G. von Scheele of Visby, Sweden, upon their arrival in Lindsborg in November 1901, at the Union Pacific Railroad station. The Scheeles had come to participate in the twentieth anniversary celebration of the founding of Bethany College. The Brases at the time were newlyweds of only six weeks.

Daisies abound on the Bethany College campus in the early days.

VI.

Hagbard Brase and the Lindsborg "Messiah" Tradition

A feeling of great anticipation prevailed that Palm Sunday evening, March 28, 1915, as chorus and orchestra members quietly took their places in the well-filled auditorium to present the 91st performance of Handel's *Messiah* by the Bethany College Oratorio Society. A new organist, Ellen Strom, was seated at the console of the organ. The orchestra tuned up under the direction of Arthur E. Uhe, concertmaster, who was serving for the first time in that capacity with the society. The four soloists, Ethyl Coover, soprano, Ida Gardner, contralto, Arvid Wallin, tenor, and Thure Jaderborg, bass, all members of the Bethany music faculty except Gardner, took the stage amidst momentary silence. Then, as the chorus and orchestra arose to greet the new director, thirty-eight year old Hagbard Brase took his place at the podium, bowed to the audience, turned and smiled at the members of the chorus and orchestra. As he picked up the baton for the "Overture," he began a distinguished career as the inspiring leader of the oratorio society for the next thirty-one years.

A full consensus prevailed in the selection of Brase as the director. Dr. Ernst F. Pihlblad, President of Bethany College, expressed his evaluation and that of many others when he wrote: "We are pleased that Professor Hagbard Brase was chosen as director of the Bethany College Oratorio Society. We have known Professor Brase for many years as a sterling musician, who on the basis of his comprehensive knowledge of his art, gained the respect and admiration of his colleagues and he should be regarded as a godsend in his role as a superior chorus leader. Although quiet and reserved by nature, he has

51

the unique capacity to inspire enthusiasm among his singers. It is a well-established fact that Handel's immortal oratorio has never been performed as masterfully by our oratorio society as during the recent Holy Week performances."[1]

There were other enthusiastic responses to Brase's first year as director. *The Lindsborg Record* expressed the sentiment of the community as follows: "Never has a conductor gone to his desk more eminently fitted for his trying task than Mr. Hagbard Brase. He knows what he wants and in a quiet, unobtrusive manner proceeds to obtain it for his organization.... We have it from competent critics, who heard the concert last Sunday night and have listened to renditions in recent years, that the chorus showed decided improvement. The shadings and the pianissimo effects are most perfect while nothing has been lost in the tremendous climaxes."[2]

Lindsborgs-Posten also praised the chorus and the leadership of the new director: "It is no exaggeration to say that the chorus never sang better than last Sunday evening. As a chorus leader Hagbard Brase is in his element. In both his personal talent and broad musical knowledge he is the man for the place. He has brought out new resources in the chorus that one had no idea were possible."[3]

In the audience of the Easter Sunday performance of *Messiah* was Mme. Johanna Gadski, famous star with the Metropolitan Opera Company, who had presented a magnificent recital that afternoon. Brase must have been pleased when two days later he read in *The Kansas City Star* the response that Gadski had given to a reporter's question about the Lindsborg chorus: "One of the best choruses I have ever heard." Then the reporter asked: "For a small town in Kansas?" "Nothing of the kind," was the reply from Gadski. "You need not, will not, qualify it," exclaimed the charming daughter of the diva, who came to her mother's assistance. "That's it," said Gadski. "We will not qualify it. It is one of the best choruses I have ever heard. Stop."[4]

The auspicious beginning by the new director and chorus continued the next year. The response in *The Kansas City Star* provided a symbol of what was to be the pattern across the years: "The performance was distinguished by the brilliant work of the chorus. Director Brase wins from his 500 singers splendid tone volume closely massed and showing effects of long ensemble practice. The climaxes are impressive and subtleties have developed through thirty-five years of "Messiah" singing." James Harrod, New York tenor, added his compliments by stating: "Next to the Handel and Haydn Society of Boston, the Lindsborg "Messiah" Chorus is the finest I have ever heard."[5]

Lindsborg was in the midst of its annual Music Festival April 1–8, 1917, when the news came on April 6 that the United States was at war with the Central Powers. *The Lindsborg News-Record*, had described the situation and tension that prevailed prior to the declaration of war by recounting developments in the Palm Sunday concert a few days earlier. Following the last "Amen" of *Messiah*, "the atmosphere was electrifying as 2500 voices sang *America* to the accompaniment of the Bethany Symphony Orchestra and the handclapping of 5000 hands brought a climax which would linger in the memory of everyone present." When Brase turned to lead the chorus and audience in the singing of *America*, a large United States flag from a window in the dome was suspended before the audience. The newspaper then concluded: "It was a tribute to the flag that had never been witnessed or heard before." This was the zenith of a great day. In the afternoon Galli-Curci had thrilled the packed audience "with such singing Lindsborg had never heard and which Lindsborg never again hoped to hear until Galli-Curci returns."[6]

Although World War I brought great changes to American life, the "Messiah" tradition with its abiding spiritual message continued to inspire singers and music lovers. However, the wide-spread influenza epidemic caused the 1918 Music Festival to be postponed from Holy Week to May 5–12. A full schedule of events was maintained with Olive Fremstad and Lucy Gates as the celebrity artists. The 100th rendition of *Messiah* was presented on the first Sunday of the festival. Minnie K. Powell, writing in *The Kansas City Star*, described the performance as follows: "Even the oldest inhabitants of Lindsborg, a city of a hundred "Messiah" concerts, admitted that the hundredth given last night surpassed all predecessors. Always a well trained body, the chorus of 500 sang its jubilee with a freshness of feeling and a depth and brilliancy of tone that proclaimed its reverent love of Handel's monumental work."[7]

On May 13, 1918, immediately after the conclusion of the annual festival, a special Union Pacific train of eleven coaches brought the chorus and orchestra to Camp Funston, near Junction City, Kansas, for two performances of *Messiah* at the All Kansas Building for members of the 89th division which was scheduled for action in Europe. The invitation was financed by five Kansas City, Missouri, business organizations and *The Kansas City Star*.

The performances at 4:00 p.m. and 8:00 p.m. were unique in the history of the chorus as the members sang for rows upon rows of men in khaki who filled to capacity the 4,000 seat building. In the evening hundreds of soldiers stood outside since all seats were occupied. The long established Lindsborg tradition of no applause at concerts did not prevail. The chorus received sustained applause which required them to arise again and again. Across the landscape of the military reser-

vation resounded the majestic music describing Him "Who is King of Kings, Lord of Lords, Wonderful, Counsellor, the Mighty God, the Everlasting Father and Prince of Peace." The Air, "Why Do The Nations So Furiously Rage Together" by the bass soloist, was repeated [at the evening performance] because of unceasing applause. As a grand finale Director Brase led the chorus, orchestra and audience in a stirring rendition of *The Battle Hymn of the Republic*. It had been a day of great inspiration and as the weary chorus entrained for the small community in Central Kansas, it was with a prayer that God would add His blessings to the listeners and performers.[8]

The renditions at Camp Funston were the only appearances of the oratorio society outside Lindsborg since the early 1880s when the chorus sang *Messiah* at Salemsborg, Fremont, McPherson, Assaria and Salina and in 1883 at Rock Island, Illinois. The year 1922 provided for performances at Oklahoma City, Oklahoma, and Kansas City, Missouri.

On February 8–9, 1922, the 114th, 115th and 116th renditions were

society appeared for the first time in Kansas City. It was the seventh time that renditions
during the first year of 1882. Except for that first year, Dr. Brase was the conductor of
Kansas City rave reviews were outstanding, and the society was invited back to that city
traveled for a twelfth time, when a "Messiah" rendition was presented for the first time

given at Oklahoma City under the sponsorship of the Oklahoma State
Teachers Association. A special train transported the members of the
chorus and orchestra. *The Daily Oklahoman* reported that not in many
years had there been such an outpouring of people as filled the 5,000
seats of the new Coliseum. The music critic described the performance
as follows:

> For those who heard the Bethany Chorus and assisting artists sing
> *Messiah*, the performances fairly exceeded anticipation. It was an event
> so beautiful and inspiring as to be no less than epochal. The extraor-
> dinary vitality of *Messiah* has survived a good many well-meaning but
> unsatisfactory performances. And therefore it is all the greater joy and
> satisfaction to hear it sung in all its pristine and undiminished vigor
> as it was given Wednesday night.[9]

The Oklahoma City Times also expressed enthusiasm for the results
produced by Director Brase and the Society:

> Director Brase seems to know how to place his singers to give a per-
> fect tonal balance—a balance so perfect that all seemed like one great
> voice. Not once did he lose control of this one voice concept. His precise

beat brought out the inspiring seriousness of the work; his knowledge of his forces made his fortissimos effective and altogether pleasurable to hear. Only unlimited praise can be showered upon the Lindsborg organization for its beautiful choral work.[10]

In November 1922 the oratorio society again presented *Messiah* outside Lindsborg. On November 18–19 the new American Royal building, Kansas City, Missouri, provided the setting for audiences that numbered 10,000 at each performance. *The Kansas City Star* described the performance enthusiastically: "The chorus scored a triumph....The effect was a revelation.. ..The great tonal mass was as flexible as the tone of a coloratura soprano, tender in quality, fluent, sinking readily in the shadow and flaming out as easily into a burst of tone. The manner in which voice answered voice as one, sopranos, contraltos, tenors, basses, each a tone in the fully colored mosaic, led those who admire great singing to listen at times purely for the technique's sake."[11]

Director Brase's mastery of the "Messiah" score came to a real test when during the singing of the first chorus he broke his eye glasses upon which he depended for full vision. However, there was not the

The Ling or "Messiah" auditorium was the third home for the oratorio society, and it was replaced in 1929 by Presser Hall auditorium.

smallest pause as the rendition continued without interruption.

The Sunday performance was especially appreciated by the audience and music critics. *The Kansas City Star* reported the following: "Yesterday's audience...heard an inspired performance. Listeners were obviously thrilled and hung on every word of the chorus that came from the little town of Lindsborg to set a new standard of oratorio singing in Kansas City.... There was more than splendor, more than faithful study and fine musicianship behind the choral passages as they were sung yesterday. There was splendid exaltation and the fervor that is only possible when the difficult music has been so carefully studied that it has become easy for the singers." The writer concluded by referring to the great applause at the end of the concert when the chorus arose again and again in response to the plaudits of the thousands of listeners: "Director Brase was too modest to show that he knew it was for him. Perhaps he did not realize it, for a man so singularly devoted to his ideals could overlook the fact that he was in every note the chorus sang, all of him, body and soul."[12]

The oratorio society's enthusiasm and that of the audiences steadily increased under Brase's capable and inspiring leadership. Moreover, he exerted sustained efforts to enrich the quality of the performances. In 1922 more exacting voice tests were required in order to be certain that the prospective singer would be able to make a vocal contribution. Brase also developed a systematic method to provide appropriate notations on the scores of the books used by the singers. Many of the copies were marked personally by the director in red pencil, thus creating more certainty for the singer's responsibility. The number of persons seeking membership increased substantially. When a *New York Times* reporter visited the campus during the rehearsal season of 1923 he was informed that 764 singers had applied for membership. Approximately 150 were required to wait for vacancies that might occur in the next year.[13]

An important development in enriching the quality of the chorus occurred in 1925 when Brase started rehearsals of selected choruses and chorales of Bach's *The Passion of Our Lord According to St. Matthew*. Although later pages provide detailed information about this important development, which resulted in annual performances on Good Friday of *The St. Matthew Passion* beginning in 1929, it is appropriate in this context to identify this action as an important phase in the ongoing enrichment of performances.

When more than four decades of the singing of *Messiah* at Lindsborg had been recorded, *The New York Times* in 1923 recognized the past and made a prophetic statement about the future: "The singing of *Messiah* at Lindsborg at Eastertide every year is becoming somewhat of a national institution.. *Messiah* will go on and one can safely predict that when another forty years has gone by, *Messiah* will still be sung—sung until it is what the people of Lindsborg think it is— the American Oberammergau."[14]

The great success of the oratorio society stimulated recognition of the need for a new music auditorium. Closely associated as an integral aspect of this achievement was the need of the excellent School of Music for better instructional facilities in the form of studios, classrooms, ensemble areas, etc. The octagonal college auditorium, dedicated in 1895, had served well as a multi-purpose building for more than three decades but the frame structure had limited seating arrangements and the new age and situation called for modern facilities. In the course of time the result was Presser Hall, which *Étude*, the well-known music journal described as "One of the finest music buildings in America."

Dr. Ernst F. Pihlblad, President of Bethany College, Dean Oscar Lofgren of the College of Fine Arts, Director Hagbard Brase, Treasurer Jens Stensaas, G. N. Malm, dedicated Lindsborg resident, and others had dreams about a new music auditorium and instructional building. The "Messiah" concerts in Oklahoma City and Kansas City in 1922 produced the first specific funds for this purpose. In 1924 a successful general campaign for funds for Bethany College to the amount of $300,000 was conducted within the Kansas Conference of the Augustana Lutheran Synod, in the Lindsborg community and among alumni and friends. In 1926 Mme. Schumann-Heink, who had sung recitals to packed houses in 1913 and 1916, sang a benefit concert for the proposed new music hall saying, "America has no other Lindsborg. I want a hand in this one." Marion Talley, a prominent young soprano, Kansas City, presented a benefit concert in 1928.

The combined efforts resulted in the dedication of the music auditorium during festival week in 1929. Groundbreaking ceremonies had brought Prince Wilhelm of Sweden to Lindsborg in March 1927. In June 1929 President Pihlblad made the joyous announcement that Francis J. Cooke, distinguished president of the Presser Foundation, Philadelphia, had informed him that the foundation would provide $75,000 to aid in constructing the studio and classroom section. The entire complex was appropriately named Presser Hall.

When the singers and friends of the oratorio society walked on the Bethany campus in the gathering twilight of Easter Sunday evening, April 8, 1928, they saw the rising walls of the new building on their way to the octagonal frame "Messiah" auditorium, known later as Ling Gymnasium. It was a time of farewell, so to speak, as they gathered for the 139th and last performance in the building in which *Messiah* was heard for the first time in 1895. This was a time of remembrance for many people that balmy April evening. A few had sung or heard *Messiah* performances for thirty-three years in this building. In addition to Hagbard Brase, five others had shared leadership responsibilities there: N. Krantz, Sigfried Laurin, Samuel Thorstenberg, Earl Rosenberg and H. C. Malloy. In recent years the oratorio society had included Bach's *The Passion of Our Lord According to St. Matthew* in autumn rehearsals and in the performance of selected choruses at Thanksgiving time. The membership of the chorus had increased from 143 in 1895 to 437 in 1928.[15]

The auditorium had been a unique cultural center for celebrity concerts as Max Muller has described them in his interesting and comprehensive book, *Prairie Carnegie: The Story of Presser and Ling* (1977). Since 1895, famous artists, constituting almost a "Who's Who" in national and international music circles had performed there, generally during the "Messiah" Festival. Included among them were Nordica, Ysaye, Pablo Casals, Gadski, Schumann-Heink, Galli-Curci, Olive

Presser Hall includes the large auditorium still in use, facilities for the Bethany College music department, and numerous other academic and administrative offices.

Fremstad, Mischa Elman, Frieda Hemple, Erika Morini, Erna Rubenstein and others.

Although there were remembrances of famous artists and previous performances of *Messiah*, attention that Easter Sunday evening in 1928 was focused on the final rendition in the old auditorium. *The Lindsborg News-Record* stated that "The crowd that gathered around the auditorium was tremendous. Every seat had been sold and people were buying 'standing room only' tickets. Hundreds were outside who could not gain admittance." The newspaper then wrote its final story about the last concert in the auditorium:

> When the final "Amen" of the "Amen Chorus" signaled the end of *Messiah* Sunday night, it also marked the final use of the old building for the Festival.... The chorus, which sang so wonderfully Sunday night, sang with mixed joy and sadness—joy when thinking of the fact that a new building will await them next year and sadness when they realized that they were singing *Messiah* for the last time within the old building. The audience was likewise aware of the drama of the occasion. Never has an audience listened with such attention and such interest as the audience of Sunday night displayed. The farewell concert in the old building was a memorable performance.[16]

This final rendition in the old auditorium was also a memorable occasion for Hagbard Brase. He had conducted the oratorio society there for thirteen years and the excellence of the performances had received national attention. Local newspapers expressed their appreciation for his leadership. *Lindsborgs-Posten*, in the context of the farewell performance, printed the following: "*Messiah* was performed as usual but with a special festive atmosphere brooding over the building so rich in memories. The chorus sang under Professor Brase's leadership with such overpowering strength and enthusiasm as if to emphasize the meaning of this farewell. Never has our chorus obtained such artistic perfection." The writer observed that it was with great sadness that he missed the chorus' long-time secretary, Gustav Nathaniel Malm, who had passed away in February. *The Lindsborg News-Record*, after calling the performance "memorable in the annals of the society," concluded by stating that "Hagbard Brase directed with inspiration, blending the chorus and orchestra into a perfect unit of majesty and power."[17]

When Hagbard Brase raised his baton for the 140th rendition on Palm Sunday 1929, it was in the new Presser Hall auditorium with its fine stage, chorus seating, and audience capacity of 2250. A warm spring day and a great influx of music lovers made it a glorious occasion. *The Lindsborg News-Record* described the event as follows: "The chorus and orchestra were on their mettle, realizing that the first rendition in the new building would set a precedent for the future. The great body rose to the occasion. Hagbard Brase directed with fervor and authority that was most convincing." The oratorio society now had a fine music temple. Richard Crooks, famous tenor, had been presented in a concert during the afternoon.[18]

Palm Sunday 1929 introduced a full week of concerts and special events. On Good Friday afternoon a dedicatory program featured a special cantata, *Pilgrims of the Prairie*, music by Carl Busch, text by E. W. Olson. The composer conducted the performance by the oratorio society although Brase had led the rehearsals. Good Friday evening witnessed a memorable event, long dreamed about and planned by Hagbard Brase—the first annual Good Friday performance of Johann Sebastian Bach's *The Passion of Our Lord According to St. Matthew*. The soloists were Marie Montana, soprano, Mrs. Raymond Havens, contralto, Ernest Davis, tenor, and Stanley Deacon, bass. Arvid Wallin was at the organ. Arthur E. Uhe served as concertmaster. There were 2500 people in the standing room audience for the Easter Sunday evening performance of Handel's oratorio. The transition to the new auditorium, later to be known as Presser Hall, had been made.

The oratorio society in 1929 and 1930 had extended seasons of performance. Two renditions, with Hagbard Brase conducting, were presented in 1929 at Convention Hall, Kansas City, Missouri, in December, under the sponsorship of the Kansas City Chamber of Commerce. This was a special Christmas activity in recognition of the message of *Messiah* in the spirit of the season. Members of the oratorio society willingly shared in this enterprise which generated funds for aiding in financing the studio and classroom section of Presser Hall. More than 500 members of the chorus and orchestra traveled by special Union Pacific train to Kansas City on December 12 for the performances on December 13–14. More than 14,000 people were in attendance at the two concerts.

The renditions were enthusiastically received by the audience and music critics. Luigi Varani of *The Kansas City Journal-Post* wrote about "the great performance" presented with such "magnificence." He observed further: "No doubt the result is accomplished through devotion coupled with innate passion for art and artistic expression.... There are times when the singing is electrifying. It is as if all these men and women, young and old, collect all the splendor of their heritage, bringing to it their store of love, beauty and magnificence to the celebration of the rite." The critic then discussed the role of Director Brase from a technical point of view: "The dynamic scheme was extraordinary. Even in the bigger bursts of sound there was a sense of measure and the spirit of beauty was never lost for all the volume.... It was good to see the structure lineature brought out and the harmonic and countrapuntal clarity being maintained. Tender were the phrases in "Worthy Is The Lamb," while "All We Like Sheep" had brilliancy. And never before, it seemed, have the heavens opened up as they were to the volleying "Hallelujahs" of last night."[19]

The music critic's response in *The Kansas City Star* was introduced by the headline, "Lindsborg Chorus Scores a Triumph in Kansas City." The following compliment for the achievement of the director, soloists, orchestra and chorus was presented: "Nothing could have been finer than the 'Hallelujah Chorus' of yesterday. Its clear attacks and releases of brilliant tone are a marvel to a listener. The 'Amen Chorus' was a rich tonal tapestry, breathing the spirit of redemption." The review concluded: "To Dr. Brase's splendid musical training and ideals the choir owes its rank among the great choruses of the world."[20]

The "Messiah" performances in Kansas City in December 1930 were successful although the total attendance for both concerts of 9,000 was considerably below that of the previous year. The impact of the economic depression was being felt.

The decade of the 1930s, the fifth in the oratorio society's history, added a new chapter of praiseworthy achievement. Although the serious economic conditions and dust storms characterized the early years of the decade, the interest of the singers and the quality of performances continued at a high level. An article in *The Kansas City Times* presented an enthusiastic appraisal of the 1933 Easter Sunday rendition of Handel's oratorio: "As the twilight of a perfect Easter day spread over the little prairie town, 2500 persons assembled from far and near to hear the Bethany Chorus sing Handel's *Messiah* for the 153rd time. The chorus has risen to superlative heights but never in the memory of those who have heard the chorus sing, heard it sung with more inspiration and with more organ-like precision of tone. The choruses were sung with a joyous zeal becoming an Easter performance. The inspiration prevalent in the chorus was caught by the soloists."[21]

The beautiful day described above was in sharp contrast with Palm Sunday two years later. *The Kansas City Star* indicated this vagary of nature: "The day dawned clear and peaceful. The early rays of the sun played upon the golden cross of the steeple of the old Bethany Church, etching it against the sky as a token of a benediction resting over the little cultural center of the Southwest." Then all was suddenly changed: "Soon a dark cloud was seen sweeping toward Lindsborg. Within five minutes the sun was hidden.... The storm grew more intense."[22]

The writer then reported the response that was given to nature's

The Bethany College Oratorio Society is under the baton of Dr. Hagbard Brase in Presser Hall auditorium.

interruption: "The handicap of the storm seemed to challenge the members of the chorus who, under the hand of Dr. Brase, gave one of the most inspiring renditions of *Messiah* ever given on Palm Sunday afternoon. The voice of the chorus was exceedingly responsive to the slightest wish of the director. The dynamics were finely graded.... The chorus was in good voice in all its passages, excelling if anything in the climactic 'Hallelujahs.' One thing that impressed the audience was the joyous quality in the voice of the chorus even though the storm was raging outside Presser Hall and it was so dark that afternoon that all the lights had to be used."[23]

When Director Brase and members of the oratorio society left Presser Hall that stormy Palm Sunday in 1935, he and many of them recalled Easter Sunday, April 2, 1920, and the *Messiah* performance that day. A snowstorm of blizzard proportions unloaded so much snow that drifts were piled high. Many singers and ticket holders found it impossible to travel over snow blocked roads. Pablo Casals, world famous cellist, was scheduled for a concert that afternoon. He, his wife and accompanist were stranded at the Union Pacific railroad station in Salina. However, train officials resolved to open the tracks to Lindsborg for an excursion train. Two large snow-plow engines attacked the huge drifts with the result that the train whistle sounded the note of victory. Casals presented a magnificent concert to the great delight of the listeners. *Messiah* was sung well that evening but with fewer singers and listeners than usual.[24]

Brase and the members of the oratorio society were pleased to receive immediately prior to the 1935 festival a letter from the famous Handel and Haydn Society, Boston, through George F. Halch, secretary, in which Alma Swensson, co-founder of the Lindsborg society, Director Brase and members of the chorus and orchestra received greetings and best wishes from the oldest oratorio society in the United States. The Boston organization was celebrating its 120th anniversary. In addition to the traditional singing of *Messiah*, the Handel and Haydn Society had introduced *The St. Matthew Passion* to the United States.[25]

Dr. Pihlblad often spoke about Bethany College, including its musical traditions, on regional radio stations.

Dr. Emory Lindquist, president of Bethany College is at the WDAF radio microphone on Palm Sunday of 1945, while Kansas Governor Andrew F. Schoeppel awaits his turn in the background.

The later 1930s witnessed the appearance of potential dark clouds of war upon the European horizon although the storm did not strike with its full fury until September 1939, when the Nazis invaded Poland. In faraway Kansas, life continued its normal course temporarily. The Lindsborg festival continued its full program of events. *The Kansas City Star* described the performance on Easter Sunday evening 1938 as follows: "Tonight's rendition was an inspiring one from every point of view. The chorus, for which Handel's musical difficulties long since have ceased to be a problem, sang the big ensemble numbers with something more even than its oldest friends have learned to expect. Responding without fail to every indication from Dr. Brase's vigorous beat, they moved with ease and precision through the intricate patterns of contrapuntal sound." The critic praised the balanced mass tone and pointed out that "the chorus was equally responsive to the restrained passages, where, as in the pianissimo close of 'All We Like Sheep Have Gone Astray,' more than 400 voices blended together in a finespun web of chords not unlike the effect of *Lohengren's Prelude* played by the strings of a highly trained symphony orchestra." *The Musical Courier* stated that the oratorio society on Easter Sunday, April 12, "gave an inspired performance of Handel's music in Presser Hall."[26]

Once during the 1930s the oratorio society performed elsewhere than in Lindsborg. In April 1934 a special train brought the chorus and orchestra to Wichita for two performances of *Messiah* at the Forum. Only one rendition had been planned but since it was sold out so quickly, another one was scheduled. *The Wichita Beacon*, after commending the chorus for fine performances, also assessed the role of Director Brase: "No small element of the chorus' success resided in the experienced and mature baton of Hagbard Brase. It seems fitting that in the deeply religious nature of the music, Dr. Brase should be more than a conductor but a leader and a source of inspiration to the chorus. In these varied capacities Dr. Brase evokes from his people a clarity and fullness of meaning that makes Lindsborg's *Messiah* an outstanding and unforgettable experience."[27]

The decade of the 1940s, with the tragedy and demands of World War II, soon made an impact throughout the United States although the grim implications were not fully realized until the Japanese bombed Pearl Harbor in December 1941. The military draft prior to the declaration of war made some impact upon the membership of the tenor and bass sections of the chorus, but the serious consequences were not felt until after 1942. There was anxiety immediately prior to the "Messiah" Festival week in 1941 because Dr. Brase had been ill in his home for several days. On Palm Sunday, however, he was at the

In November 1945 as part of the Salvation Army's 80th anniversary held in Kansas City, the Bethany College Oratorio Society sang excerpts of Messiah in the Municipal Auditorium of Kansas City.

podium. The local newspaper wrote: "Dr. Brase was an inspiration to the singers and players throughout the concert. Under his guidance the chorus added another magnificent performance, revealing once again the power, the shading, the confident approaches to the technical requirements of the work that have made the society famous."[28]

Blanche Lederman, representing *Musical America*, was in Lindsborg for the 1941 festival week. In the April issue of the well-known national music journal she referred to "Bethany's incomparable oratorio chorus" and then presented the following evaluation: "Under the masterful, deeply inspired direction of Dr. Hagbard Brase, who for twenty-five of the organization's sixty years has instilled in the famous group high traditions of choral singing, the performances on Palm and Easter Sundays defy adequate description. It is a stirring, unforgettable experience to hear the Bethany Oratorio Society sing the Handel work." She also reported that Gregor Piatigorski, accompanied by Pavlovsky at the piano, won resounding applause "for a superlatively performed concert of 'cello literature in the afternoon prior to the oratorio rendition."[29]

During the week March 29–April 5, 1942, the sixtieth anniversary of singing *Messiah* at Lindsborg was observed but on a fairly modest scale because of World War II. Special guests were ten members of the original chorus which presented the first performance at Bethany Church, Lindsborg, in March 1882. A full program of events was enjoyed during the week. *The McPherson Daily Republican* observed appropriately: "The world has changed across the decades but the eternal message of Handel's great oratorio still inspires men and women with its beauty and majesty. Hagbard Brase directed the chorus, now showing the impact of World War II, since fewer young men sang. Their places were filled for the duration by older singers who responded to the emergency situation. An innovation was the singing of the first stanza of the national anthem by the chorus and audience prior to the rendition of the oratorio."[30]

The 176th performance of *Messiah* was sung in Presser Hall for 1700 members of the 94th infantry division of the United States Army stationed at Camp Phillips, near Smolan, Kansas, and some airmen from Smoky Hill Air Force Base, south of Salina, on April 21, 1943. Military vehicles lined up four abreast in front of Presser Hall as military personnel came to hear Handel's oratorio. The soloists, orchestra and chorus performed beautifully under the direction of Dr. Brase to the large and appreciative audience.[31]

On Easter Sunday 1944 one of the two largest audiences to have heard the Handel oratorio in Presser Hall, more than 2500, with hundreds turned away, shared in a fine performance. People stood around the seated listeners both upstairs and downstairs. This rendition was dedicated to the memory of individuals closely identified with the oratorio society whose lives had come to an end since the last festival. Those memorialized were Alma Swensson, co-founder and widow of Dr. Carl Swensson, Dr. Ernst F. Pihlblad, former President of Bethany College for thirty-seven years, and charter members Mrs. N. O. Carlson, Mrs. Matts Johnson, and Anna Swenson.[32]

The concert in 1944 was also dedicated to 600 former members of the chorus who were then serving in the armed forces of the United States at home and abroad. As the "Messiah" message was sung there were remembrances of the past and prayers for near and dear ones, many of whom were facing danger in a world at war. The bass solo, "Why Do The Nations So Furiously Rage Together?" had special meaning to those who sang and listened that Easter Sunday evening in Lindsborg. Since the performance was recorded and broadcast by short wave radio across the seas by the United States Office of War Information, members of the chorus and audience shared a feeling of fellowship with loved ones far away.[33]

The Easter Sunday performance that year brought out the best in the chorus and orchestra. The results were greeted with high praise.

The Salina Journal used the following unique approach in commending the director and chorus: "A warm smile of approbation from Dr. Brase is a token of esteem those who follow his baton covet—unless the whole performance is right, the smile is missing—and well do the singers know it. But on Easter Sunday 1944 Brase's smile of approbation was present."[34]

Only one more festival, that of 1945, remained before World War II came to an end. Illness prevented Dr. Brase from conducting the Palm Sunday performance that year. Arvid Wallin, longtime organist and friend of Brase, directed the oratorio society that day. Hagbard Brase conducted the Easter Sunday performance.

In November 1945 a ten-coach Missouri Pacific special train transported members of the chorus to Kansas City, Missouri, for participation in the eightieth anniversary celebration in Convention Hall of the founding of the International Salvation Army. More than 10,000 people filled the hall to listen to a gala program which included speeches by General Evangeline Booth, daughter of William Booth, founder of the organization, General George C. Marshall, Chief-of-Staff of the United States Army, selections by the Kansas City Philharmonic Orchestra and the Bethany College Oratorio Society, Dr. Hagbard Brase, conductor. The chorus sang five selections from *Messiah*. Since service in World War II had decimated the Bethany orchestra, The Kansas City Philharmonic played the orchestral accompaniment. Arvid Wallin was the organ accompanist. The chorus selections were enthusiastically received by the audience. Members of the orchestra and others expressed their esteem for the effective manner in which Dr. Brase brought together the chorus and orchestra with gratifying results following only one brief rehearsal.[35]

The sixty-fifth annual "Messiah" Festival April 14–21, 1946, was Hagbard Brase's finale as director of the oratorio society. When he put down his baton after the last "Amen," concluding the 183rd rendition on Easter Sunday evening, the silence of the moment yielded to sustained applause in acknowledgement of a splendid performance. Members of the chorus, orchestra and audience did not know that this was Dr. Brase's last performance as director. If it had been known, this would have been a highly charged emotional occasion. The announcement of his resignation for reasons of uncertain health came in August. It was accepted with deep regret but also with full understanding.

When Dr. Brase closed the large copy of the *Messiah* score on the podium April 21, 1946, he concluded a distinguished career as director since 1915. Over a period of thirty-one years he had conducted ninety-two performances of *Messiah*. He had introduced and conducted annual Good Friday renditions of the *St. Matthew Passion* since 1929.

Tributes to Dr. Brase's great achievement are many and laudatory. Included in a most personal manner is the spoken and unspoken gratitude of a few thousand former members of the oratorio society and a host of listeners to the performances. Many newspapers and periodicals have recorded for posterity the high esteem in which contemporaries held him as a person and conductor. The following comments from local, regional and national publications are representative of a larger number.

The Lindsborg News-Record expressed the community's appreciation: "A large amount of the credit for the continued excellence of the rendition of Handel's masterpiece by the oratorio society is Dr. Brase, who through his understanding, persistence, humor and thorough knowledge has gained the loyalty of the chorus members, strengthened their belief in the tradition of the *Messiah* and helped them put forth their best efforts so that the renditions of the Lindsborg oratorio society have become so widely publicized as exceptional. The common love of good music has united Dr. Brase with the community and the people love and respect 'their' director of the 'Messiah' Chorus."[36]

Clyde Neibarger, well-known music editor of *The Kansas City Star*, spoke for a wider area and a larger public when the news came that Dr. Brase would no longer conduct the Lindsborg "Messiah" Chorus: "The news of Dr. Brase's retirement from the directorship of the Lindsborg "Messiah" Chorus comes to the editor of this department to arouse a deep sense of personal regret. For more than twenty years he has seemed to be a notable example of a certain type of Old World music master that is becoming extremely rare. He brought to his position a superb classical background and technique but with it a complete and steadfast devotion that one finds in these times only in the story of Bach's residence in Leipzig or von Bulow's labor for the Wagner theatre in Munich. Under Dr. Brase's leadership the Lindsborg chorus rose from a prairie congregation to a world famous institution, in its latter days widely traveled and internationally broadcast." The music editor then concluded with this tribute: "And so deep was his concentration that so far as giving any outward sign, he never seemed to be aware that he had become a national figure or that his chorus had gained rank and fame among choral groups."[37]

When Howard W. Turtle, in *The New York Times*, wrote about Dr. Brase and the "Messiah" tradition at Lindsborg, he described the quality and ultimate meaning of the oratorio performances: "When Brase begins his stern beat for one of the great choruses of *Messiah*, he draws from the chorus a body of tone that is truly magnificent in its splendor. It is an expression in song of voices schooled to near perfection

More than one national magazine printed this photograph of Dr. Brase as the Bethany Oratorio Society conductor.

through years of training. But it is more than that." The writer then concluded his evaluation as follows: "In Lindsborg the "Messiah" is religion—as much as the Swedish peoples' worship at the church services which they attend every Sunday.... So when they sing their oratorio it is more than a performance of music quality. It has behind it a conviction of truth; of high purpose; of religious zeal that lifts its ecstacy to the sky and resounds in countless 'Hallelujahs.' "[38]

Handel's oratorio, as performed by the Lindsborg chorus, has been heard by radio listeners intermittently since 1922. In that year WDAF, the broadcasting station of *The Kansas City Star*, transmitted the performance on Sunday afternoon November 19 from the American Royal Pavilion in Kansas City, Missouri. Radio station KFBI, Abilene, Kansas, made available several choruses from *Messiah* in April 1933 to listeners in Kansas and elsewhere in the Plains area. The Blue Network of the National Broadcasting Company (NBC) provided for hundreds of stations the rendition of eight choruses from Handel's work on Good Friday in April 1939. Telegrams and letters of appreciation were received by Dr. Brase and the society from all parts of the United States and Canada. A similar national broadcast was presented by the Mutual Broadcasting Company in the following March. Palm Sunday 1945 initiated a series of live radio broadcasts from Presser Hall of complete performances of the *Messiah* by WDAF, the radio station of *The Kansas City Star*. Recordings of performances on Palm Sunday 1944 and 1945 were transmitted around the world by the United States Office of War Information.

Although Dr. Brase's service as director of the "Messiah" Chorus ended with his retirement in 1946, circumstances brought him once more to the podium during the Palm Sunday performance in 1948. Erma Young, who was in the audience, described this unexpected development in *The Kansas City Times*: "A human drama moved in to intensify the emotion of today's presentation of Handel's *Messiah* by the Bethany College Oratorio Society, when Dr. Hagbard Brase, 70, retired conductor, was called from the audience to take the baton after Arvid Wallin suffered a fainting spell. The chorus was singing 'Behold the Lamb of God,' when Wallin, leaning heavily against the conductor's stand and with great courage succeeded in completing the number. Lloyd Spear, concertmaster, assisted Wallin to a chair in the orchestra section. Mrs. Wallin came immediately from among the sopranos. Her husband whispered to her, "Call Dr. Brase."[39]

The writer then described what followed: "There was a stir through the audience a few seconds later, when white-bearded Dr. Brase, for thirty-one years the guiding hand of *Messiah* presentations, walked briskly down the aisle toward the platform. Stepping to the music stand, the veteran conductor picked up the baton, turned to the appropriate page in the score, gave the down beat and the music was resumed. The selection was the aria, "He Was Despised," with Vivian Bauer as soloist. Wallin then conducted three choruses after which he relinquished his post, and sat with the orchestra while Dr. Brase concluded the remainder of the oratorio." When the "Amen Chorus" was completed, there was a resounding ovation as Professor Wallin and Dr. Brase, close friends and long-time colleagues, took a bow together.[40]

One important factor was not known to the members of the audience and oratorio society. Dr. Brase was wearing his "distant vision" glasses and not the "close vision" type that he used while reading a music score. He turned the pages at the proper time and conducted the numbers from memory. This was a remarkable achievement of the veteran and knowledgeable conductor.[41]

VII.

Singing the "St. Matthew Passion" and Other Sacred Song

Although the Lindsborg chorus had included Mendelssohn's *Elijah*, Haydn's *Creation* and other oratorios in occasional performances, only Handel's *Messiah* was sung annually. In the early 1920s Hagbard Brase contemplated the addition of a major oratorio to the regular repertoire. A great admirer of the works of Johann Sebastian Bach, he was interested in *The Passion of Our Lord According to St. Matthew*. In addition to his esteem for the music and message of this oratorio, he was aware of the coming 200th anniversary of the first performance of the *St. Matthew Passion* at St. Thomas' Church, Leipzig, on Good Friday 1729. Moreover, the year 1929 would be the 100th anniversary of Mendelssohn's production of Bach's oratorio in Berlin. A commemorative rendition at Lindsborg on Good Friday 1929 seemed singularly appropriate and possible. His dream was destined to become a reality.

Brase realized fully how much the *St. Matthew Passion* would enrich the Holy Week festival, but he was also interested in what the singing of the more difficult Bach oratorio would mean in the development of the chorus. Although he knew that the *St. Matthew Passion* was composed for a small choir and orchestra, he believed that rehearsals and renditions by a large chorus would be meritorious. He expressed this belief as follows: "A chorus that sings only one oratorio regularly needs variety and the challenge to greater achievement."[1]

The decision to introduce the *St. Matthew Passion* has an interesting background. Since Dr. Brase realized fully that the composition was difficult and especially so for a large chorus, he decided in 1920

that the singers should be introduced to Bach's music by rehearsing
Sleepers Wake, a cantata thirty minutes in length. The Bach composition was performed on Good Friday during the "Messiah" Festival
of 1920.

An interesting source for the development of the Bach tradition at
Bethany College is found in a statement by Dr. Brase quoted in *The
Kansas City Star* in April 1920: "I feel that Lindsborg is the place for
the chorales and cantatas of Bach to be sung. Ours is a Lutheran community, familiar with ancient chorales and hymn tunes which the
master used as foundation themes for his cantatas....The groundwork
for giving these chorales to Western America belongs especially to us
by reason of our long study of *Messiah* and our knowledge of the original hymn tunes."[2]

The writer in the Kansas City newspaper then described the problem that confronted Director Brase in introducing the chorus to Bach's
cantata: "It was even hard at first to discern the tune for it moved
slowly in the midst of the fugal variations, but it moved, and the singers recognized the familiar themes in spite of the splendor of the contrapuntal flights." The result was also described: "After a season of
study, the music was sung with a measure of success on Good Friday
evening. Something of the dignity and massive power of the work was
communicated to the audience, although at least another year of study
will be required before the limpid fluency of Bach's music will be satisfactorily reproduced."[3]

When the *Bethany Messenger*, the student newspaper, discussed the
introduction of the Bach cantata, which it heartily applauded, the editor wrote in both a practical and prophetic manner: "It is to offset
the insinuation that the Lindsborg chorus is capable only of singing
Messiah and to prove its proficiency in singing other compositions that
this plan of rendering a Bach cantata has been instituted. If that plan
is continued from year to year there is no question but that the chorus
will gradually develop a reputation of Bach renditions equal to that
which it has for the *Messiah*."[4]

The performance of *Sleepers Wake* showed substantial improvement
on Good Friday evening the following year. On each occasion the rendition of the *Messiah* was shortened in order to make time available
for the Bach work. Two years of singing Bach's cantata had convinced
the director and chorus members that Bach's works could be included
in the oratorio society's repertoire through patient and sustained rehearsal. Hagbard Brase awaited the proper time for introducing the
St. Matthew Passion.

After much reflection and discussion with his colleagues and members of the chorus, Dr. Brase made the decision that the *St. Matthew*

Passion would be sung by the oratorio society in 1925. The response was mixed; some people applauded with enthusiasm while others wondered if the singers would assume responsibility of extra rehearsals and if the public would attend the concerts. Brase was supported by Dean Oscar Lofgren, members of the music faculty and many members of the chorus.

Fortunately a manuscript copy of Brase's notes for a speech (no date) about Bach and the *St. Matthew Passion* is available. It is presented here as an indication of his view and the challenges in rehearsing and performing this oratorio. At the outset of the lecture Brase described the form and structure of Bach's composition and then he presented his evaluation of the music and message.[5]

The Passion of Our Lord According to St. Matthew
by Johann Sebastian Bach.
Notes by Hagbard Brase.

The St. Matthew Passion requires very complicated resources for its performance. It is written for two choruses, two orchestras, organ, harpsichord and from four to six soloists. The text is taken from the 26th and 27th chapters of the Gospel of St. Matthew. The story is sung by a tenor soloist who is called the Evangelist. The words of Jesus are sung by a bass and the parts of the High Priest, Peter and Judas should be sung by another bass. In addition to the text from the Gospel, there are hymns sung to chorale melodies and free poems set to music, called arias and ariosos. The chorus represents sometimes the disciples of Christ, at other times the Jews and on many occasions, it represents the Christians, often called the Christian congregation. *The St. Matthew Passion* was performed for the first time at Leipzig as a part of the main service for Good Friday. It is divided into two parts, the first part sung before the sermon and the second part after the sermon.

The composition begins with an introductory chorus. This introduction is often referred to as the "Daughter of Zion," the singers calling to each other—"Come ye daughters, share my anguish." From time to time the Christian congregation enters with the chorale, "O Lamb of God, most holy." This chorus is not only very long and complicated, but what is more important, is that it is an expression of the most passionate sorrow and anguish. Bach seems to have meant that we are not only to witness a tragedy, not only to be spectators, but that we are a part of this tragedy, and the cause of it.

I think we could read the 26th and 27th chapters of the Gospel of Matthew without receiving any deep impression because we are too familiar with the story. But when listening to Bach's treatment of the text we realize that it is stupendous drama where human iniquity and wickedness seem to be victorious. This drama is described in music with constantly growing power from the institution of the Eucharist to the death and burial of Jesus. The story is often interrupted by chorales or arias of a contemplative nature. These interruptions occur after the more dramatic moments in the drama. It is as if the spectator, the Christian congregation, must at these moments give expression to its pent up emotions.

The St. Matthew Passion is not only for the musician or the chorus singer; it is one of the musical works that has impressed many people, especially churchmen. Among the many opinions I could cite I will select only one which is truly remarkable. Archbishop Nathan Söderblom of Sweden was not only a learned theologian but much interested in music. He and others considered *The St. Matthew Passion* to be such an important document that it was called the fifth Gospel and a new revelation.

Söderblom has written in one of his books after having studied Bach's *Mass in b minor* and *The St. Matthew Passion* that he had gained a deeper understanding of the Incarnation and Redemption. This seems difficult to understand until we realize that music addresses itself to the feelings and not in the first place to the intelligence. Perhaps we do not believe a truth until we can feel it. Music speaks to the heart, and the Bible admonishes us to believe in our hearts or with our hearts. Martin Luther knew something about this when he said that music was next in importance to theology.

It has not been my intention to speak in detail about the music of *The St. Matthew Passion*, but I wish to say a few words about the last two choruses. After the death and burial of Jesus the music changes— there comes a stillness over it. It is as if Bach intended to take us to the grave of Jesus and this is what he musically speaking does. In Leipzig, where Bach lived, it was customary at funerals, after the rites at the grave, that some friends of the deceased would step forward and say a few words of appreciation. Bach used this custom in selecting the form for the next to the last chorus. It is now the Christian congregation that is gathered at the grave. Each of the four soloists sing a short sentence expressing the beliefs of the church. After each solo the believers sing the words, "Lord Jesus, rest in peace."

The St. Matthew Passion begins with a chorus full of sorrow, anxiety and despair. The last chorus beginning with the words: "Here yet a while, Lord Thou art sleeping," could be called a chorus of resignation. There is longing and sorrow but no despair. There is even the assurance that the grave is not the end, but that "It shall become a welcome portal, leading man to life immortal."

It is said that Bach throughout his life, even from early childhood, had a longing for death. It seems rather peculiar because he was a very strong and robust man. But whenever he composed music to words that have to do with death, resurrection and immortality, he seems to be more than usually inspired. And in this last chorus he gives not only a very inspired expression of the resignation felt by the friends of Jesus at the grave, but also of the Christian hope in the resurrection and in the immortality of believers.

In September 1925 members of the Lindsborg chorus were invited to assemble for the first rehearsal of *The St. Matthew Passion*. Calmly and deliberately Hagbard Brase talked about Bach's oratorio—the great music, the abiding spiritual message, his belief that the chorus could rise to the challenge of singing well the choruses and chorales, that extra effort would be rewarded by achieving this worthy goal. His enthusiasm and the confidence of the members in their director brought a good response.

The rehearsals during that first year culminated in the performance of several selections from the *St. Matthew Passion* at Thanksgiving time. The program of twenty-one selections included ten chorales and choruses. A small beginning had been made in faith. *The Lindsborg News-Record* wrote appropriately: "The Bethany College Oratorio Society has taken a forward step last Sunday evening (November 22) in rendering some selections of *The Passion of Our Lord According to St. Matthew*." The writer observed that "the large audience present was agreeably surprised by the progress that had been made." The singers were complimented for having attempted and accomplished a task that few choruses could duplicate.[6]

Dr. Brase's courageous leadership in introducing Bach's oratorio was also recognized by the editor of the community's newspaper: "Bethany College and the oratorio society are fortunate in having a director of Mr. Brase's ability. He directs with fine understanding and assurance bringing forth the musical content with a true appreciation for the text which lends cohesion and symmetry to the interpretation. The chorus sang well Sunday night, coming into its own in the stately choruses and the last number was beautifully rendered." The soloists, Irene Houdek, soprano, Katherine Penner, alto, Benjamin Tillberg, baritone, all Bethany faculty members, Roy Campbell, tenor, Wichita, Arthur E. Uhe, concertmaster, and Arvid Wallin, organist, were commended for their fine contribution to the performance.[7]

In September 1926 the oratorio society continued rehearsals of *The St. Matthew Passion*. The performances of selected numbers occurred again at Thanksgiving time. *The Lindsborg News-Record* described it as "very good, even better than last year," although regret was expressed that there were not enough tenors and basses to balance the women's voices. The writer felt that "the opening chorus is stupendous in its demands, being written for double chorus, double orchestra, organ, and in addition, a children's chorus which was composed of pupils from the seventh and eighth grades of the public schools." In the opinion of the writer, "the best work of the oratorio society manifested itself in the last chorus which was given with beautiful flowing voice production and expressive appeal which touched all hearts profoundly." The article concluded with high optimism: "The concert was a success and it is gratifying to feel that a foundation has been laid for a true appreciation of the immortal work of the great genius, Johann Sebastian Bach."[8]

After four seasons of rehearsals and partial performances, Brase was ready to present a more complete rendition of *The St. Matthew Passion* on Good Friday evening, March 29, 1929, during "Messiah" week. The director's dream had become a reality. This was the 200th anniversary of the first performance at St. Thomas' Church, Leipzig, with Bach conducting. Sharing with the chorus and Director Brase in the rendition were the members of the orchestra, Arthur E. Uhe, concertmaster, Arvid Wallin, organist, and the soloists, Marie Montana, soprano, Mrs. Raymond Havens, contralto, Ernest Davis, tenor, and Stanley Deacon, bass.

This great musical event in the history of the college and community took place at the same time as a variety of events related to the dedication of Presser Hall, as previously described above. This resulted in less attention and recognition being given to the distinguished achievement of introducing *The St. Matthew Passion* to the Bethany and Lindsborg religious and cultural tradition. However, *The Lindsborg News-Record* assessed the implications in the following comment: "Friday night the oratorio society made history when the first official performance of Bach's *The St. Matthew Passion* was presented to the public for the first time. The big city newspapers had heralded this rendition as an occasion of the greatest musical importance in the Middle West." A later generation, after more than half a century, can testify to the authenticity of the local newspaper's prophetic vision.[9]

The fears of those who believed that singing *The St. Matthew Passion* would be opposed by many members of the chorus did not become a reality. Four hundred members formed the chorus for the performance of selected numbers of the Bach oratorio in November 1925 following the season of new and special rehearsals. The membership of the chorus during the previous April for the "Messiah" Festival of that year had been 435. However, 460 singers formed the chorus the following year. When the first more complete performance was presented during Holy Week 1929, the chorus consisted of 472 singers. The data show an increase of interest by singers during the critical period.[10]

In April 1933, Minnie K. Powell, music editor of *The Kansas City Star*, presented a status report on the Lindsborg Bach performances of this early period: "Of paramount importance to music lovers of this region is the annual Good Friday performance of Bach's *The Passion of Our Lord According to St. Matthew* at Lindsborg....All who have

attended the Good Friday concerts at Lindsborg within recent years
have been greatly moved by the contrapuntal power of Bach's music
and the thrilling beauty of the Bethany College Choral Society's performance under the direction of Dr. Brase."[11]

An article by Guy Criss Simpson, in *The American Organist*, September 1939, presented an interesting review and a current evaluation of singing *The St. Matthew Passion* at Lindsborg. His initial observation set the stage for what followed: "There is a greater reason
than the "Messiah" tradition why Lindsborg deserves praise; it is the
only town, large or small, west of the Mississippi River, which has
given Bach's *The St. Matthew Passion* every year since 1925." Moreover, he pointed out that this unique distinction could include a larger
area than the above. The article then described the decisive factor in
this splendid development:

> This record is due largely to the zeal and persistence of one man, Dr.
> Hagbard Brase, director of the Lindsborg chorus.... Long before he ven-
> tured a public performance of *The St. Matthew Passion*, Dr. Brase in-
> troduced the work bit by bit, to his chorus. The reception was mixed

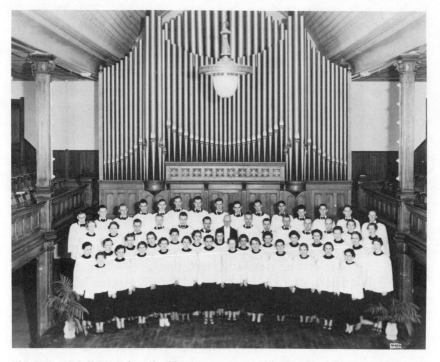

*The Bethany College A Capella Choir was organized by Hagbard Brase in 1935, and
the first concert tour was taken by the choir shown above in the spring of 1937.*

and success was not at first fully assured....Since 1929 the work has been given every Good Friday to steadily increasing audiences.

The critic in *The American Organist* then discussed a vital phase of development by candidly discussing strengths and weaknesses of the Bach performances:

> And how does the Lindsborg chorus really do the *St. Matthew Passion*? Not perfectly, of course, but with astonishing finish and with deep understanding of the religious significance of the work. Five hundred singers are too many, the fine edge of the contrapuntal line becomes blurred....but in a community enterprise it would be impossible to eliminate any regular chorus members when this work is given.

The writer then concluded his comment: "As it stands, the chorus is not overpowering in volume; a lovely floating quality of tone is its chief characteristic. The chorales are taken very slowly, with deep devotional feeling. The effect is ineffable....I have traveled to Lindsborg five times to hear the St. Matthew's and each time I have been moved by the music."[12]

Progress continued to be made in the performance of Bach's oratorio as Director Brase developed the resources of the chorus and orchestra. The following commendation appeared in *The Kansas City Times*, in April 1938: "The chorus was singing with fine tone and precision, giving excellent balance to the complicated interlocking phrases. The soloists showed unusual command of their difficult roles, and gave not only full musical but full spiritual value to their texts. The orchestra trained to its best by Professor Arthur E. Uhe, furnished fine and dependable support, sustained by the individual experience and skill of Arvid Wallin, the society's veteran organist. The result from first to last has been the revelation of the complete success of what for the first years has been considered a daring experimentation in Western oratorio history."[13]

The Bach performance in 1941 was the last prior to the full impact of World War II. The local newspaper was pleased with the result: "The performance of the chorus, orchestra, organist and soloists under the direction of Dr. Brase was one of the finest by the Lindsborg organization....The chorales were beautifully done Friday night and the shorter, dramatic chorus numbers were given more expression. The heavy double choruses received splendid interpretation." The writer also expressed appreciation for "the orchestra's outstanding work and the individual musicians who were heard in obligato parts. Arvid Wallin was splendid in the big role given him by the music."[14]

The St. Matthew Passion renditions suffered more from the impact of World War II than those of *Messiah*. The demands upon the orchestra were greater in the former than in the latter. Moreover, the absence of many male singers who had developed considerable ability in singing the tenor and bass parts, created some problems. The determination to continue the Bach tradition, even in modified form, was sustained. In 1943 an abbreviated performance was presented. Sixteen choruses and chorales were sung. The continuity of the message was supported in a measure by using the spoken word of the text with the Reverend James Claypool as narrator.[15]

The Bach performance did not regain its full stature until the rendition in 1946. It represented the best possible effort in the context of the losses of singers and orchestra players during the war years. Radio station KSAL, Salina, Kansas, initiated live broadcasts of the *St. Matthew Passion* in the middle 1940s.

The tradition established by Dr. Brase has been sustained and enriched in a gratifying manner. The response of the singers and orchestra members and greater audience participation prove that the faith and vision of Hagbard Brase and his associates have been productive. Recent performances under the direction of Dr. Elmer Copley have witnessed the transformation into reality of the hope expressed by the founding director that in the future *The St. Matthew Passion* would join *Messiah* in twin excellencies of oratorio performance in Lindsborg.

Intimately related with the commemoration of the 250th anniversary of the birth of Johann Sebastian Bach, a special program devoted

The interior of Bethany Lutheran Church, shortly after 1904.

to the great composer's works was presented at Bethany College in February 1935. Included were selections by a choir organized and rehearsed by Hagbard Brase. This singularly important background resulted in the formation of the Bethany College A Capella Choir.

The first full concert by the choir of more than fifty voices was May 27, 1936. *The Lindsborg News-Record* expressed its pleasure as follows: "The concert was characterized by balance and fine musicianship. The attacks were precise and the crescendos and diminuendos smooth. The audience was in a receptive mood and showed how keenly they enjoyed the entire program. The applause was spontaneous and enthusiastic."[16]

A good beginning had been made under the leadership of Hagbard Brase. In 1937 the choir made a successful tour in Nebraska, Iowa, Missouri and Kansas. Later tours included Colorado. The response of listeners was enthusiastic and a tribute to the director and singers. The repertoire of the choir included works by Bach, Bortniansky, Kastalsky, Glinka, Lotti, Fischer, Tschaikowsky, Sibelius, Grieg, Gretchaninov, Roman, Williams, Cain, F. Melius Christiansen and a composition and an arrangement by Brase. The design of the house program by Lorena Daeschner (Mrs. George Hall), a student in the Bethany Art School, was in the form of a pen and ink drawing which showed the interior of a cathedral, quite likely that of Skara. This was a symbol of what the choir represented in its message to listeners.[17]

In the third season of the choir's history national recognition came to the organization in the award of second place in the Choral Quest sponsored by the Columbia Broadcasting Company. Each of more than twenty choirs across the nation presented a half hour concert over the network facilities of CBS. The Bethany Choir sang compositions from its regular repertoire through the facilities of radio station KFH, Wichita, Kansas, for broadcast over more than 100 outlets.[18]

The entries in the Columbia Choral Quest were judged by outstanding musicians and critics including Deems Taylor, Dr. John Finley Williamson, founder and director of the Westminster Choir, Princeton, New Jersey, Davidson Taylor, director of the music Division of CBS, Ward French and Fredrick Schang of Columbia Concerts. In a letter to Brase Dr. Williamson wrote as follows: "The work that you are doing with the choir is delightful and the singing of your group was splendid. I congratulate you and your choir upon this work."[19]

When Dr. Brase wrote to Louis H. Diercks, director of the Ohio State University choir, to congratulate him upon winning first place, the Bethany director received a reply which praised the "fine singing of the Lindsborg choir" and the following personal compliment: "Your most kind note of congratulations ...has meant more to me than any note that I have received. How I envy your students to have as a leader a man of such character."[20]

The Bethany Choir appeared in national radio broadcasts during the next two years, over the CBS network in 1939 and through the stations of the Mutual Broadcasting Company the following year. Many radio broadcasts were presented over KSAL, Salina, and over other Kansas and out-of-state facilities in the succeeding years, when the organization was on tour.

A successful tour was made by the choir in 1940. Large audiences greeted the singers and director at various places. *The Reporter-Herald*, Loveland, Colorado, presented its readers in April 1940 with a thoughtful and complimentary review of the performance there: "The complete control of Dr. Hagbard Brase, veteran and artistic director of the organization, gave Loveland music lovers an example of unusually excellent choral technique. Modulations effected in the difficult numbers amazed the large crowd as did the completeness of the repertoire....Perfect pitch of the a capella group was maintained in every one of the numbers in a flawless presentation. Perhaps the outstanding number was the *Beautiful Saviour* arrangement by Christiansen. The contrasts and modulations of Dett's *Listen To The Lambs* was one of the finest interpretations ever heard in Loveland."[21]

Activities of the choir were considerably curtailed after 1942 until the end of World War II because of an insufficient number of male singers. A women's choir directed by Dr. Brase provided additional choir opportunities. More normal activities were resumed after 1945. Elmore Carlson served as student director at times during this period to assist Dr. Brase. This organization was the responsibility of the veteran conductor until he asked to be relieved of the assignment in 1948.

On Good Friday afternoon 1951 more than 100 former choir members returned to the campus in order to pay a tribute to their former esteemed director. When the last number of the program, *After Holiday*, composed by Brase, was to be sung, the audience arose as he was called to the stage by Ralph Harrel, conductor and a former pupil. A stirring and emotional rendition of Brase's fine composition by former and current members brought the program to an impressive climax. Dr. Brase was then presented a monetary gift and a "Book of Memory" with greetings of those students who had sung for him. Each of the singers received a copy of *After Holiday* to commemorate the occasion and to cherish as a remembrance of a fine person and musician.[22]

Hagbard Brase served as organist and director of the Bethany Lutheran church choir from 1921 to 1943. He always sought to maintain high standards. He was opposed to the so-called "program emphasis"; music sung by the choir should be a vital part in the continuity of the worship service and not separate from it. The repertoire included the finest English and Swedish anthems. Members of the congregation and visitors shared the privilege of listening to Dr. Brase's excellent and beautiful improvisations on the organ. His studies at the Royal Conservatory of Music, Stockholm, had provided a splendid background for this creative achievement. There is great regret that recordings are not available of his improvisations.

When Hagbard Brase's request for retirement as director of the church choir was granted, the congregation at the annual meeting on New Year's Day 1944 expressed the deep gratitude of the members in a statement which concluded with the following words: "Recognition is given for his faithfulness, his professional skill and his personification of the best and the highest in the church music tradition and in promoting appreciation for it."[23]

On April 4, 1954, the year following Dr. Brase's death, the 40-member church choir, with Professor Rolf Espeseth conducting, presented Dubois' *The Seven Last Words of Christ* in a memorial tribute to their former director. The house program contained the following message. "It is fitting at the approach of Holy Week that we pay tribute to the undying memory of Hagbard Brase, whose talents were dedicated to music and thereby to the spiritual inspiration and sustenance of those to whom church music and the stirring message of Holy Week means so much. Dr. Brase lived, and his spirit still lives, so that 'The glory of the Lord shall be revealed' and that 'Blessing and honor and glory and power, be unto Him that sitteth upon the throne, and unto the Lamb, forever and ever."[24]

VIII.

Conducting, Teaching and Composing

CONDUCTING

Hagbard Brase is best known by a large public as a conductor with special reference to the Bethany College Oratorio Society. His view of the responsibility for conducting the "Messiah" Chorus is outlined in the manuscript of a lecture on that subject. In it he sets forth his basic emphasis which is in part narrated in the sections that follow. Brase began his lecture by underlining the importance of rehearsal:

The supreme business of a chorus is the rehearsal....The success of the rehearsal depends almost entirely upon the preparation that the conductor gives to it. He must know how much time he can devote to the different numbers or to the different topics. Otherwise he may be tempted to spend more time in working on certain portions of the music that he happens to like or experiment with some pet theory.... In fact the whole rehearsal season ought to be planned beforehand as far as this is possible.[1]

The Bethany director believed that "at the first rehearsal the work, or part of it, should be gone through repeatedly until the singers are fairly familiar with the music. There should not be too many interruptions at the outset. Singers will not profit by corrections until they are quite familiar with the music. When they have some knowledge of the score, they will welcome corrections and the real work of the chorus can begin."[2]

Hagbard Brase's approach to a variety of aspects in preparing a large chorus is described in the following language:

It is often impractical at the beginning to give an oratorio chorus formal exercises in correct breathing, tone placement, blending voices, intonation, etc. But the conductor will find many occasions when some instruction in these matters can be given. For example, if a word is badly mispronounced, the conductor can point out how impossible it is for a part to blend if even only a few singers use a wrong pronunciation or a different tone color from the rest. A few minutes can then be spent in singing the particular phrase in which the mistake occurred. A convenient pitch should be selected so that the whole chorus can take part in this exercise. When at all practical it is good policy to keep all the singers working at the same time, even when a correction is aimed at a particular part.[3]

A series of vital topics—correct breathing, intonation, good attacks and good releases, means of expression, choral tone and the basic elements of a good choral singer, were discussed in that order. Attention was given first of all to correct breathing:

The importance of correct breathing cannot be stressed too much.... What the conductor can expect in the matter of breathing is that the singers learn to breathe deeper than in ordinary conversation and that they learn to conserve the breath as much as possible. Amateur singers are apt to sing too many tones in one breath and should be told to breathe and not allow themselves to run out of breath. The leader should insist that all singers take breath together at convenient places. In the management of sustained chords or extended runs where no break should occur, the singers should be told to breathe several times, taking care to come in again in the correct pitch and with the same tone color. If the desired result of evenness is not attained by this method, the part can be divided in sections, each section taking breath in different measures.[4]

Attention was then given to intonation. He pointed out that there are several causes of faulty intonation—wrong methods of breathing, inadequate posture, physical tiredness, lack of mental alertness and a faulty ear. The lecturer pointed out that there is one cause of poor intonation that is often overlooked. Singers are told to sing on the vowels which, of course, is correct. But in words beginning with certain consonants it is very important that the pitch is introduced through consonants. Carelessness in this respect often leads to wrong intonations.[5]

Brase devoted considerable attention to good attacks and good releases, which present difficulties in a large chorus. One factor is attention and discipline. If this is pointed out, a marked improvement can be noticed almost immediately. He suggested the following: "A good attack can sometimes be procured by having the singers breathe with the baton on the beat preceding the entrance of a part. I find it harder to teach a chorus good releases than good attacks. It seems that the average chorus singer is reluctant to let go of a tone once he or she has gotten a firm hold on it....Good releases are somewhat allied both to staccato singing and to phrasing and the larger the number of singers with good musicianship in the chorus, the greater the success should be in securing really musical releases." He also believed that it was helpful to use "catch phrases" in instructing the chorus. Instead of suggesting that the singers begin together, ask them to "hit the note in the middle;" instead of talking about the desirability of finishing together, tell them "to cut" or "to cut it short." Singers easily associate such expressions with the desired method of singing and much time is saved.[6]

Hagbard Brase then discussed the balance of parts: "In singing a fugue for example, the tenors may lead off with the subject, to be followed by the altos, with the answer only a fifth higher. Coming after the penetrating tones of the tenor part, the alto part may and often will produce almost an anticlimax." He suggested a remedy for this situation. "A section of the soprano part can be called upon to sing with the altos, which will give the alto entrance its required brilliancy." He recalled a place in the "Amen Chorus," of *Messiah*, where Handel gave the theme to the tenors so low that it was entirely ineffective. Brase then asked a dozen or more basses to sing with the tenors at that particular place. He proposed the same approach in other choral works but it should be done with discrimination.[7]

In compositions involving imitative singing he felt that much time could be saved if the whole chorus sang in unison the particular theme to be imitated. The conductor would thus have an opportunity to correct mistakes in breathing, phrasing and diction and the entire chorus would receive the benefit of the instruction. At the least sign of tiredness or absentmindedness of the members, the conductor must return to the music and continue the rehearsal.[8]

The importance of expression in oratorio singing received quite detailed attention.

> The most important means of expression are f [forte] and p [piano], crescendo and diminuendo. We have all heard the expression—take care of the pp and the ff will take care of itself. Like many popular sayings it contains a half truth. I would like to put it this way: take care of the pp [pianissimo] and the mf [mezzo forte] will take care of itself, ...Both pp [pianissimo] and ff [double forte] must be practiced and both take a great deal of concentration on the part of the singers. Choruses are often able to sing fine diminuendo and where it seems to me that many fail it is in the management of crescendos. I believe that the reason is that the conductor starts them too soon... If a crescendo is started not very far from its highest peak it generally can be carried out with good effect....In executing a crescendo I find it helpful to tell a chorus that the word means "start soft," and in singing a diminuendo I explain that it means "start loud." It works.[9]

The Bethany choral director presented his views of factors in producing good choral tone, which he recognized as "a fascinating subject but one that will take considerable time." Short exercises on different vowels were recommended in connection with a particular phrase in the composition. He further suggested that if special exercises were introduced in order to improve the tone, the conductor must be sure that the desired results are obtained. It will be harmful if the singers feel that the directions lead nowhere and that time has been wasted.[10]

The concluding section dealt with the qualities of a good choral singer. He quoted F. Melius Christiansen, famous former conductor of the St. Olaf College Choir, that "the best choir singer is the one who can produce the strongest tone without being heard individually." A good singer will know when not to sing, for instance, when the high notes for some reason are defective, when the neighboring singers sing too loudly in a pp passage, and when the singer will never sing an ff progression so loud that he or she cannot hear the other singer in the same part. Morever, he cited the positive qualities of a good singer: "The eyes will be kept on the music during the rests and on the conductor when singing. A good singer knows that he or she is personally responsible for the success of the performance, but in partnership with the conductor as a more experienced and directing member of the enterprise."[11]

The skill and technique of Hagbard Brase was deeply appreciated by those who were associated with him in various relationships. Lambert Dahlsten, organ professor and long-time organist with the oratorio society, has written: "Hagbard Brase's conducting was highly skilled not only because of his natural ability but also as a learned thing. He had a 'technique.' His conducting was of the 'pin point' variety. His performing groups always knew what he meant by what he did with the baton. The 'downbeat' and the 'release' were defined. This is also true in organ where release is as important as the attack. The transfer, musically speaking, from organ to vocal and orchestral performance, is thus a natural one." Lloyd Spear, who served as concertmaster and later as director of the oratorio society, has high esteem for Dr. Brase as a conductor: "He had one of the most beautiful clear beats I have ever played under or witnessed. The oratorio rehearsals were a joy. Dr. Brase was always well prepared. His instructions to chorus and orchestra were always concise and clear. He was skilled in maintaining the correct tempo. He was a master in controlling the large group. If there seemed to be lack of effort or concentration, the members of the chorus and orchestra were soon made aware of it and the pattern was changed. He had a unique, quiet and forceful way of communicating his desires to the performers."[12]

Ralph Harrel, like Spear, a former Brase student and director of the oratorio society, and also an admirer of his mentor, recalls how impressed he was when as a member of the chorus he participated in rehearsals and performances: "Dr. Brase was surprisingly gentle considering the amount of work to be done with such a large chorus of amateurs. After several weeks of rehearsals (twice weekly) the chorus misinterpreted the gentleness and succumbed to laziness, and something had to be done. About three weeks before Palm Sunday as I recall it, something happened within Dr. Brase, and for an instant he would show fire and anger in his eyes and voice. Suddenly the chorus would come to attention, and for the next three weeks the rehearsals seemed to sail toward the performances with gratifying results."[13]

One day when Dr. Brase was discussing conducting with Ralph Harrel, the former made a humorous statement relating to the way a conductor looks and feels on the podium. Brase's figure was such that he seemed to be pretty much all arms and legs. He always had suits made by C. A. Berggren, the excellent Lindsborg tailor. The statement that Harrel remembers from that discussion was the following: "A few years ago I had Berggren make me a new suit of tails and I have conducted much better ever since."[14]

Elmore Carlson, who was thrilled to sing in the oratorio society under Dr. Brase's leadership and esteemed those experiences later as a member of the Boston Handel and Haydn Society, served as a student assistant to Brase in the activities of the a capella choir. He has written about this pleasant relationship: "I remember the intensity of preparation for rehearsals and concerts. The director always stressed the fact that not until the music was memorized, and the words to be sung came from the heart, would we really be ready to sing. He was able to bring out the various dynamics with a minimum amount of motion and facial expressions. He was a master of interpretation and was able to make members of the chorus understand the words and music. Dr. Brase instilled in me, a student director, the need to 'feel' the music, not just to beat out time or rhythm."[15]

Hagbard Brase worked hard in preparation for rehearsals and performances. The scores of *Messiah* and *The St. Matthew Passion* which he used on the podium had detailed markings on various aspects of the conductor's responsibilities. He spent much time studying and reflecting on the scores. Lambert Dahlsten has made the following observation: "One of the interesting phases of Hagbard Brase's personality was his ability to take the score of the *St. Matthew Passion* and 'hear' how it should be performed. His hearing of Bach's oratorio in Sweden many years before introducing it in Lindsborg was recreated, in my belief, when years later he conducted the Bethany College Oratorio Society in rehearsals and performances."[16]

Former members of the "Messiah" Chorus recall pleasant and rewarding experiences of singing under the baton of Brase. Only a few of that large number can be cited. Jessie Ash Arndt, has written about her first experience as a member of the chorus in 1918: "Students of Bethany College had the privilege of having membership in the chorus. The first rehearsal with that great body of singers was an unforgettable experience....I will always remember the hush of excitement as we gathered in the octagonal frame building. The organist pulled out the stops of the fine instrument behind the choral section. Hagbard Brase, conductor, came forward with a quick step and military bearing. There was a brief and cordial word of greeting and general satisfaction among the older members that the rehearsals were under way again."[17]

The new member of the chorus described then what happened: "For us students there was awe. Professor Brase tapped, motioned with his baton, and we found ourselves standing with the others in a single movement that was like the sound of a deep breath. The first number rehearsed was "For Unto Us a Child Is Born." I had never seen the score before but I sang it as though I had always known it. One could not do less than sing; one was carried on by the mighty wave of music." When decades later, Jessie Ash Arndt, then a feature writer with a well-known Boston daily newspaper, recalled her student experiences at Bethany College, she wrote: "This was Lindsborg and its 'Messiah.' There were fathers, mothers, sons and daughters, and more than one grandchild of an original member of the chorus."[18]

Rosalie Carlson Nelson, Bethany College graduate, sang in the chorus almost three decades later than Jessie Ash Arndt but there is a striking similarity in their remembrances. The former has written: "When Dr. Brase walked briskly up the ramp of Presser Hall auditorium, took his place on the podium and the beautiful notes of the "Overture" and then the tenor solo, "Comfort Ye, Comfort Ye, My People," were heard, we all sat spellbound. Soon Brase would raise his baton, *look at everyone* and expect the entire chorus and orchestra *to return that look*, and we would begin the first chorus of *Messiah*. The excitement was almost overwhelming and I can still feel the thrill of that first note coming alive under his direction. His kindness to all of us throughout the rehearsals and performances was inherent but he also had a firmness that was unmistakable and widely respected."[19]

There is unanimity of enthusiasm for Hagbard Brase as a choral director. The range is from Allison Chandler, who at the age of sixteen was accepted as a member of the chorus and sat high up on the benches near the pipe organ in the old auditorium, to Albertha Sundstrom, who has had continuous membership for more than half a century. She remembers Brase's considerate and patient attitude as well as his outstanding musicianship. These qualities were tested according to Albertha when members of the chorus began to rehearse the *St. Matthew Passion* as she recalls so well: "It seemed as if so many in the chorus were opposed to the innovation but that did not deter him." Seated next to Albertha Sundstrom for many years has been Nadine Burwell Berggren. She reports proudly: "I have Dr. Brase's photo in the front of the "Messiah" book which I have used for thirty-six years. Albertha and I talk about him a lot. He was a wonderful conductor and a Christian gentleman."[20]

The professional reputation of Dr. Brase was clearly evident in June 1915 when the Chancellor of a large university inquired as to his availability to serve in the newly created position as the Dean of the School of Fine Arts. When this situation became known in Lindsborg, a petition was circulated which soon had 140 signatures urging him to remain at Bethany College. This response is especially significant since the chorus was not active at this time of the year and prospective signators were not readily available. The petition included the following: "Owing to the inopportune time, the chorus as a whole cannot be reached but we know and trust that you will feel that in this matter we stand unanimous." A petition was also addressed to the college board of directors, urging the governing body of Bethany College to do everything possible to assure the continuation of Dr. Brase's membership on the Bethany faculty. The members of the board of directors responded with a statement of praise for Brase's services and appreciation for the loyalty of chorus members to their director. Anxiety was replaced by glad relief at the announcement that Hagbard Brase would continue as Professor of Organ and Theory and Director of the oratorio society.[21]

Illustrations of the high esteem in which Dr. Brase was held as a conductor are found in Chapter V above, which traces the development of the oratorio tradition at Lindsborg. Music critics and journalists generally described the talent and achievement of Director Brase in words of praise and commendation. Similar statements of esteem have been made by writers and members of the a capella choir and the Bethany Church Choir but the limitations of space do not permit these citations.

Choral groups outside Lindsborg sought his services from time to time. His heavy schedule of teaching and conducting generally made it impossible for him to accept these invitations. Exceptions occurred in 1931 and 1932 when he served as a guest conductor of the Northwest Oklahoma Choral Society, Enid, Oklahoma, when he conducted performances of *Messiah*. Dr. Brase had been asked to be the guest conductor for *Messiah* to be sung by the Topeka Council of Churches Chorus and he went to Topeka for a rehearsal in January 1945. However, for health reasons he was unable to carry out the assignment on February 25, 1945, and Dr. Walter McCray, a former Bethany student and a professor at Pittsburg Kansas State Teachers College, served as conductor.

TEACHING

Hagbard Brase brought great personal resources to the teaching of music. His fine musicianship was apparent in performance on the organ, in his compositions and in conducting. His native talent had been developed by hard work and disciplined thought. Thorough and longtime study of the history of music, with special reference to Johann Sebastian Bach, had enriched his resources for teaching in classroom and studio.

Music was the central interest in Hagbard Brase's life. His views about its role found expression in various forms. On one occasion he wrote: "Music is no doubt the most beloved of all the arts and the most widely used. In spite of this it is the least understood of them all. Its physical nature, if I may use that term, is well understood. It rests on mathematics and accoustics, but we do not need to know anything about that in order to perform or listen to it. Psychologists and physiologists can tell us that we react to it mentally and bodily but they are not capable of explaining how or why we react to it."[22]

Moreover, Dr. Brase cited other aspects of music: "We do not know why some people are influenced more than others by musical sounds....The same music produces different emotions in different people.... Music has almost a mysterious power to influence our imagination and to make certain ideas seem true. Music has no message for a shallow soul. No one is very likely to acquire a deeper understanding of music unless he lives some kind of spiritual life."[23]

Students soon understood what Dr. Brase was seeking for and from them. Nelouise Hodges Stapp recalls vividly his approach to teaching: "I remember him walking to the blackboard to write harmony examples in his distinctive musical notation. He would show that chord successions could be awkward by moving the voices in certain ways. Then he would slip in another example which seemed to be exactly right. At that point we would be asked to open our books and there we found a rule which told us exactly what he had demonstrated. It seemed so proper because we had seen examples that didn't work and we needed no further proof of why that rule was important." Lloyd Spear also recalls clearly theory classes with Hagbard Brase: "He would stand in front of the class at the blackboard and contrapuntal writing almost seemed to flow from the chalk. Then he would go to the piano and play it for us. He could have been a great composer if time and circumstances had been favorable."[24]

Doris Seth Ylander studied organ and advanced theory with Hagbard Brase. Her memories of him are summarized as follows: "I admired him very much and I always felt in the presence of greatness in each encounter." When Doris had occasion to contact him following graduation, he was always responsive and helpful. On one occasion Dr. Brase sent her a bibliography of music publications which he thought might be helpful to her as a teacher. Doris was gifted in composing—one of her compositions, *The Lord Is Righteous*, was sung at the Bethany baccalaureate service in 1950. Her former theory teacher often encouraged her to develop this talent. When her first child was born, he urged her to compose a lullaby. This continuing interest in former students was characteristic of Hagbard Brase.[25]

Although Brase's theory classes were difficult and required much time for student preparation, the results were gratifying. Eloise Perry Dale found the courses in harmony and counterpoint "very inspiring." How she wished that she could go to the piano and harmonize melodies with the ease with which her teacher accomplished this task! Della Brown Crawford "never stopped being amazed at the way Dr. Brase could write chords in the Harmony II class." Nadine Burwell Berggren remembers the situation when she took counterpoint privately from Dr. Brase: "I think that he had a blood clot in his leg so I went to the Brase home where we sat in the living room. He would give me assignments like the following: 'Write in the style of Bach, using this theme.' I handed it in at the next session when he played it and said: 'Ah, you hear too many hymns'. Then he might say: 'Write in the style of Beethoven'. I handed it in, but again he said: 'Another hymn.' He then discussed at length with me what was essential in the assignment and gradually I understood and learned. That class was a memorable experience."[26]

Lois Wells, also a former student, has written as follows about Dr. Brase: "In this quiet, dignified gentleman there was such great vitality, warmth, knowledge, understanding and genuine concern for each of his students.... Nothing escaped his notice or sense of humor. Wagner's *Tristan and Isolde* was a favorite and those of us in his Form and Analysis class grew to love this opera as he took us through the work step by step pointing out the *leitmotiv* or musical theme associated with each of the character's emotions and ideas.... I am in-

debted to this musical giant and wonderful human being for the rich-
ness he added to my life."[27]

Ralph Harrel has similar remembrances of Hagbard Brase: "Perhaps the most vivid impression was that he always treated students
as adults and equals. His classes were free from anxiety, and there
was a gentle quality about the way he made corrections....He seemed
to enjoy his 'hallway' visits and as students we learned much from
him since he was so well read in so many fields. I recall spending
much time as a student and later as a faculty member in unplanned
encounters in the lobby of Presser Hall during which I received broad-
ened horizons and suggested avenues of thought which have meant
so much to me."[28]

Hagbard Brase's classes in theory are remembered with gratitude
by Roberta Pruitt Martin: "The composition classes were not just exercises in pedantic rote learning. They were delightful experiences in
living music, history, art and biographies of music personalities, past
and present—a wealth of knowledge with European culture mixed
with that of the United States and Lindsborg. When we complained
about the limiting use of prescribed chord progressions, etc. in our
beginning composition class, he advised us to learn the rules, practice
them until they became an automatic part of us, then forget them,
and we would find a freedom of expression in our writing that we
would not have had if we had not first developed habits of writing."[29]

Bethany students found that organ lessons with Dr. Brase were rewarding. Lambert Dahlsten was impressed among other things with
the thoroughness of his teacher: "In marking scores, organ and vocal,
it was Hagbard Brase's attention to detail that was of such great importance to him as conductor and to his organ students. My organ
scores were minutely marked as to fingering, dynamics, registration.
These 'details' were evident in other phases of his personality, personal appearance, the planning of his day and class lesson plans."
Nelouise Stapp appreciated the close attention that Brase gave to the
students' progress, discussion of repertoire and his fine musicianship.
She observed that "His fingers were extremely long and he had a span
of twelve keys. In addition to the size of his hands, I remember his
dexterity and ability to shift his fingers on the keys to achieve a perfect legato."[30]

Joanne Johnson recalls Dr. Brase's "remarkable memory." She described this aspect of her teacher as follows: "He could stand during
a lesson in the rear of Presser Hall auditorium and tell me the page
and measure that needed a different trill, which organ stop didn't sound
right and where the pedaling was faulty....Dr. Brase expected the best
and he inspired the best by being himself." Joanne remembers clearly

the conversation with her teacher prior to a scheduled concert in Kansas City. This was Brase's comment: "Are you worried about an organ you haven't tried? Take time to get acquainted with it, then relax and enjoy it—the music is the important thing." Then Joanne wrote in recounting this incident: "That has always brought me down to size ever since, something I have tried to pass on to students across the years. The music, not the performer, is foremost."[31]

Dr. Brase is viewed by his students as a dear and unforgettable person. After almost four decades, Rosalie Carlson Nelson writes: "I can still very clearly picture Dr. Brase striding on campus from the north in a gray, fairly wide-brimmed hat and a neatly pressed gray suit, with his distinguished looking white goatee carefully trimmed and always a smile for anyone whom he met and with a twinkle in his eye behind the gold-rimmed spectacles. And he always tipped his hat." Rosalie then continues: "If students were not on their best behavior upon meeting Dr. Brase, they would soon straighten out and act very proper. He was a most proper gentleman and this was reflected in anyone he met or with whom he interacted. He commanded the most profound respect and good behavior and to my knowledge I cannot remember a single derogatory statement ever made about him. He expected excellence, decency and respect and he got it."[32]

There is a united chorus of esteem from former students about Hagbard Brase's interest in them and what that concern meant throughout life. Norman Johnson, an organ student, who assisted his teacher as chapel organist, and later became a widely-known composer and music editor, has written: "I consider it one of the greatest privileges I have ever had, sitting at the feet of one of the finest persons I have ever known." In a letter to his teacher Norman wrote: "I and many other students have always loved your fine Christian spirit of understanding, your sincerity, consecration and unselfishness, to say nothing of your alertness and wit." Nadine Hagstrand Bohning is representative of others when she wrote: "Dr. Brase was a wonderful, dear man and I feel that he continued to influence my life throughout the years. He was always encouraging and whenever I have served as an organist, I have been grateful for the preparation he gave me." When in 1946 Nadine inquired if he would play the organ for her wedding with Paul Bohning, she requested that he improvise on the organ as he did so beautifully at the Sunday morning worship services at Bethany church in Lindsborg. She recounts that "Dr. Brase smiled and chuckled about the request and of course, Paul and I had lovely music to remember always."[33]

Helenmae Pearce Johnson recalls a pleasant experience following graduation when she was organist at the Strand Theater in Salina.

One of the first films she cued was Cecil B. De Mille's famous *King of Kings*. She remembers that she played with a feeling of inadequacy and insecurity. Then she writes: "Imagine my surprise when at the close of the film one evening, I felt a hand on my shoulder and I heard a familiar voice saying, 'Well done, I am proud of you!' There stood Dr. Brase. Once again that kindly knowledgeable teacher was encouraging his former student."[34]

Nelouise Stapp has the following remembrance of another aspect of her relationship with Hagbard Brase: "I sense that Bach's beliefs and the expression of them through his music were really a testament of Dr. Brase's beliefs. One felt in his presence that he had strong faith and Christian hope in the resurrection but he did not verbalize it. These thoughts were expressed through Bach and his music." Maridene Newell Lundstrom remembers Dr. Brase's love for the chorales and how he transmitted that love to her. He could somehow relate this beautiful music to life itself. She writes: "I will never forget his gentle voice in our conversations about life and death and his helpful views." Maridene observed that her teacher never used the first name of his students, but always "Miss Newell," a fact verified without exception by others. This in no way influenced adversely his splendid relationship with students.[35]

Bethany students had many occasions to share personal incidents with their teacher and some of the situations sparkled with the professor's sense of humor. Helenmae Johnson, who cherishes the fact that she majored in organ with Dr. Brase, was rather short in stature, four feet nine inches, when she enrolled at Bethany. She describes the setting by pointing out that "During a year of stretching to reach the organ pedals, I had grown two inches. When I mentioned that fact to Dr. Brase, he said: 'This is a result of my teaching that I never had before.'" Joanne Johnson has described a conversation that she had with Dr. Brase following a concert at the college by a flamboyant visiting organist. In a post-concert lesson, during which the concert was discussed, Dr. Brase made the following comment: "It seems as if the guest performer neglected to wear his Superman cape." Dr. Brase seldom if ever offered outright criticism, but this apt critique was quite sufficient and memorable.[36]

Hagbard Brase served regularly as chapel organist until later years. Prior to the daily chapel service on one occasion, students had pirated the human skeleton from the laboratory of the Biology Department and placed it with considerable skill in a sitting position on the organ bench. Shortly before the opening of the chapel service and in the presence of many students already assembled, Dr. Brase slowly climbed the ten steps to the raised platform where the organ console was located. As he approached the organ bench, and saw the human skeleton seated on it, his deep resonant bass voice, heard clearly by the students, carried this message to the skeleton: "Move over!" The chapel resounded with hearty laughter.

Margaret Bloomquist visited with Dr. Brase one day in the lobby of the Lindsborg post office. Upon learning that Dr. and Mrs. Brase planned to walk from their home to the Missouri Pacific depot after midnight, carrying their luggage, in order to board a train, she insisted that she would call for them and transport them to the railroad station. When she arrived at the home Mrs. Brase was engaged in locking up the house. After locking the front door from the inside, Mrs. Brase appeared at a window facing the front porch, climbed out of it, shut it and then said: "Now the house is all locked up." Margaret restrained her friendly laughter and Dr. Brase chuckled. No unwanted entry was made during their absence.[37]

Carol Anderson recalls vividly the day when using Carl Quarnstrom's old Model T Ford, he offered Dr. Brase a ride from Presser Hall to his home. The offer was readily accepted and Carol has written as follows about the episode: "What a sight we must have presented—a bright red Model T with brass radiator, top down. Behind the wheel a callow youth and in the passenger seat the very epitome of dignity and propriety, Dr. Brase, never looking right or left, holding the brim of his hat, gray always, between thumb and forefinger of his right hand, gazing straight ahead. When we arrived at his home, Dr. Brase alighted deliberately and thanked me gravely." Carol also remembers his teacher's patience and courtesy in theory classes, the thrill of singing in the "Messiah" Chorus and a capella choir and the kindness of Dr. Brase, who in 1952, when Carol's mother died, two years after his graduation from Bethany, sent a kind note of condolence to his former student."[38]

Brase's students shared in well-planned courses of study. Earlier developments in the music theory and organ curriculum have been described previously. In the 1920s the major in music theory and composition was enriched with a wide range of supporting courses in harmony, harmonic analysis, counterpoint, canon and fugue, musical form and analysis, composition and instrumentation. Only a few students completed the requirements for a baccalaurate degree in this area but the availability of electives in theory for majors in other areas enhanced their musical studies. A sizeable number of students completed the degree requirements in organ and a larger group chose this instrument as an elective. Beautiful degree recitals demonstrated the achievement of pupil and teacher with wide ranging repertoire. Students played a variety of compositions—preludes, fugues, sonatas and other musical forms by classical and contemporary composers. Students of Dr. Brase have served with gratifying results as church organists and as teachers in colleges and universities and in private studios.

In July 1916 Hagbard Brase was elected by the board of directors of Bethany College to the newly created position as Dean of the College of Music. He served as dean only during the next academic year. He did not like the inevitable detailed work in a dean's office. Moreover, the expectation that a dean was required to make frequent public speeches did not please him. Dr. Brase was still a full-time teacher of organ and theory and director of the oratorio society. Realistically these assignments were far too many for one person.[39]

The loyalty of Hagbard Brase to Bethany College is dramatically demonstrated in a survey of the salaries made available during the years. In 1902 the compensation was $600.00 plus meals in the college dining hall. It was not until late in the 1940s that this distinguished professor and conductor received $3000.00 for services during the academic year, the highest compensation of his career. The amount was $1500.00 in 1935-36 and $2200.00 a decade later. His loyalty is further illustrated by the fact that he declined offers for more lucrative positions elsewhere.[40]

The explanation of this loyalty, which created hardship for Bethany professors and their families, is found in the unique personal qualities of Dr. Brase and colleagues who were in similar circumstances. Their identification with Bethany College was deep seated and personal. They cherished the purpose and tradition that they had created and nurtured. They enjoyed the productive fellowship of kindred spirits in a creative and stimulating cultural milieu. There may have been some hesitancy, also, in being transplanted, so to speak, into a new and somewhat strange environment. They brought to Bethany and Lindsborg the qualities found in Chaucer's scholar as described in *The Canterbury Tales*: "And gladly would he learn, and gladly teach." They shared a feeling of satisfaction with their calling as teachers. Their identification with the cultural resources of Swedish American life and thought, in the context of Christian education, enriched that feeling of satisfaction. Succeeding generations are the legatees of their talent and devotion. The word "Gratitude" must be spelled in large bold letters when we recall the great heritage that has been left by Hagbard Brase and his colleagues.

COMPOSING

Hagbard Brase's talent as a composer was never fully developed because of his heavy teaching schedule and the demands on his time and energy as a conductor of the oratorio society, a capella choir, male chorus, church choir and other choral groups. However, as indicated previously, he composed and published a large number of selections for church choirs in early years at Bethany College. He continued composing as time permitted.

Brase's compositions in later years included instrumental and vocal numbers. *The Music News* reported in November 1915 that "Mr. Hagbard Brase has recently finished an *Adagio for Violin and Piano*. Although teaching large theory classes, he continues to compose. His compositions include many styles, such as orchestral and choral works, many excellent songs, and miscellaneous compositions for solo instruments."[41]

In April 1924 a recital of Brase's compositions by Bethany faculty members was presented. Included were *Chaconne for Piano and Organ* performed by Hagbard Brase, organ, and Oscar Thorsen, piano; *Arietta* and *Sketch a la Minuet*, Ahzelle Pruitt, violin; *I Am A Peach Tree*, *A Christmas Carol* and *Values*, Irene Houdek, soprano; and *Barcarelle* for orchestra and *Dante To Beatrice On Earth*, Irene Houdek, soprano, accompanied by a string orchestra, one flute, one clarinet, piano and organ.[42]

The *Arietta for Violin and Piano* was published by A. C. Ogren, Chicago. A music critic described *Dante to Beatrice On Earth* as follows: "Mr. Brase has offered something unusual....Rich in harmonious texture and masterly orchestrated, it surges throughout with real inspiration. It is broad in outline and operatic in character."[43]

Brase composed several organ selections. The best known are his *Arietta*, *Prelude*, and *Fugue* and *Toccata*. These works have been described as follows by Lambert Dahlsten: "The *Arietta* is a simple two-part piece with a very definite Scandinavian feel. The *Prelude*, *Fugue* and *Toccata* are splendid organ compositions. They are well composed, thorough in detail, based on the contrapuntal idea which is natural considering Brase's strong experience with the organ and his training which was polyphonic in nature. The compositions would be classified as nineteenth century Romantic rather than twentieth century in character and mood."[44]

The best known compositions of Hagbard Brase are *After Holiday* and *The Night Has A Thousand Eyes*. *After Holiday* was composed for the Bethany College A Capella Choir during the 1939-40 academic year. The lyrics are based on a poem of the same title by Florence Lind which had appeared in *The Lutheran Companion*. It is a beautiful composition which incorporates elements of the Swedish hymn, *Var hälsad sjöna morgonstund* (All Hail To Thee, O Blessed Morn), a traditional and famous hymn for matins on Christmas Day and Martin Luther's well-known Reformation hymn, *A Mighty Fortress Is*

Our God. The Night Has A Thousand Eyes, vocal solo, is a sensitive composition in the Romantic tradition.

The papers of Hagbard Brase contain a substantial collection of other compositions in various styles and forms. Roberta Martin, a Bethany College organ major, recalls with great pleasure the invitation extended to her by Dr. Brase to examine his compositions in order to select one or two for her recital. She has written about the experience as follows: "I spent not only one day in the Brase home but several fascinating days there. Lining the attic on three sides were orange and apple crates, all full of organ, choral, instrumental and orchestral compositions. The large number of compositions that I brought down were only a drop in the bucket.... Shortly before my recital he gave me two of his un-published manuscripts." Roberta concluded her observation with these words: "I cannot find the right words to describe Dr. Brase; perhaps others will do so. As an organist, composer, director, teacher, he was exceptional, superior, superb; as a man he had the wisdom and humility of the truly great. I have never met another person for whom I had greater respect."[45]

IX.

Christian Thought, Faith and Music

Hagbard Brase was brought up in the tradition of the Lutheran church in Sweden. He was baptized as an infant in the church at Råda and confirmed in the cathedral at Skara. The son of a Lutheran pastor, his future might have been quite different if his father had lived the span of normal years. Hagbard made the following comment on a likely alternative to his career in music: "If my father had lived longer ... I believe that I by this time would be a minister in Sweden soon ready for a pension. When I was born it was said that my father put me on the table and said: 'He is going to study four languages.' He meant German, Latin, Greek and Hebrew, in preparation for the ministry. How entirely different my life would have been if he had lived longer." Hagbard Brase did not become a minister but he maintained lively interest in Christian thought and faith throughout his life.[1]

At the death of *Komminister* Brase, Hagbard's mother, sister Ingegerd and he lived in the parsonage home of his Jungner grandparents where the boy was immersed in the religious practices of the family. When the grandfather died and the Brases moved to Skara, he shared in the religious life of the home and church. At *Skara läroverk* he participated with other students in the required studies in religion and in the daily religious services. Regular attendance at worship services and membership in the choir of Skara cathedral provided enriching experiences. His "Memoirs" record his great interest in religion and attendance at religious services during his student years at the Royal Conservatory in Stockholm.

The religious experiences of Brase in Lindsborg proved to be quite different from those in Skara and Stockholm. The immigrant religious life of Lindsborg had been influenced largely by Pastor Olof Olsson, founder, in 1869, and during the next few years. Olsson, an Uppsala University graduate in theology, and an ordained pastor of the Church of Sweden, was a *läsare*, a "reader," or more specifically, an evangelical Lutheran with a pietistic emphasis, who had emigrated to America in part because of his conflict with Bishop Niklas Sundberg, Karlstad. Olsson had many differences with the Bishop including conflict of opinion relative to the role of the church in personal conduct and opposition to "institutionalism" in the church which inhibited evangelical freedom as the pastor understood it. Olsson was an intelligent, dedicated and learned pastor who wielded great influence in his parish at Sunnemo, Sweden, and later in Lindsborg.[2]

Olof Olsson's *läsare* background with its low church attitude toward liturgy, vestments, special Holy Days, etc., produced a religious situation that was quite different from that which Brase had known in Sweden. There was a wide disparity between the old and the new in what has been called "the beauty of holiness" associated with Skara cathedral and the simple stone church in the Smoky Valley. However, the doctrine, hymnody and language were familiar. Some losses had occurred, and possibly some gains had been made in the adaptation of the immigrant church to the pioneer and frontier world. Hagbard Brase joined the Bethany congregation soon after his arrival in Lindsborg. He remained a faithful member throughout his life and participated in the Word and the Sacraments.

Hagbard Brase was deeply religious but not in the aggressive demonstrative manner that is sometimes incorrectly viewed as a mark of religious commitment. He had respect for the church and clergy but he was concerned with the shallowness of some aspects of popular religion. He read widely on religious subjects. His favorite authors were Swedish theologians, especially three archbishops of the Church of Sweden, who were capable preachers, devoted scholars and well-known ecumenical leaders—Nathan Söderblom, Yngve Brilioth and Erling Eidem. Brase admired Albert Schweitzer's life and work. He listened regularly to the radio sermons of Harry Emerson Fosdick and read his books. He was a regular reader of *The Christian Century*, an informed and progressive interdenominational weekly with a strong social message. His papers include many citations from the above authors and other theologians.

Special evidence of one aspect of Hagbard Brase's religious life and faith is available in a document written in Swedish by him and dated August 22, 1930. It records his remembrance of a religious experience during the previous night. He recopied the statement three years later on September 30, 1933, with the following notation: "This is a copy of the original which is in a black notebook. I desire to have more than one copy." The exact copy of the original and the notation provide clear evidence that this religious experience was of vital importance to him. A verbatim translation follows:

Last night I had a blessed experience. Depressed by sins and anguish I went to bed about 10:30 p.m. I prayed the prayer of the Prodigal Son: "Father, I have sinned against heaven and Thee and am not worthy of being called your son. Let me be like one of your hired servants." I thought further: "If I cannot come now I will never, never be able to do so." These words were spoken by Uncle Johan Linde on his deathbed. They were fixed in my memory. Further—"Just as I am without a straw of my own strength to build on." As these words went through my consciousness there descended a completely unexpected, indescribable peace of mind.

I became absolutely amazed and my first thought was: "Is this the forgiveness of sins?" "Yes," I thought, "and life and salvation." I began to pray immediately that this impression would remain. I became afraid that this peace would vanish as quickly as it had come. I thought about autosuggestion but that thought did not disturb me. The actual event was a fact.

Three thoughts occupied me during the following hour. I do not remember if I thanked God in more than a cursory manner. But I prayed that the feeling would stay with me a long time; I became almost afraid that it would vanish as I have already mentioned. I was determined that I would always remember this moment in future dark days. In the third place I could not fully understand the confidence with which I thought about the future. With what ease to live, to work, to meet sadness, illness, suffering with God as helper and friend.

I lay awake a long time and prayed almost the whole time. Peace remains still in my soul today. This happened immediately after 11 o'clock during the night of August 22, 1930. This is written the following day.[3]

Hagbard Brase's sincere, forthright and meaningful statement is self-explanatory. It is the unadorned record of a stable, thoughtful, intelligent man who shared in a personal experience of great importance. It reflects his view of the grace and holiness of God in unemotional language. He wrote thus the following day: "There descended on my mind a completely unexpected, and indescribable peace of mind....The actual event was a fact....I could not understand fully the confidence with which I thought about the future." As he contemplated the human situation, with its problems and questions, he was blessed with confidence in new spiritual resources to face an uncertain future.

In the background of Dr. Brase's special religious experience were decades of Christian education, worship, Bible reading and reflective thought. His religious resources had been enriched by long absorption with the music and text of Handel's *Messiah* and Bach's *The St. Matthew Passion* and other oratorios. As previously indicated, he had studied the Gospel texts for the church year, written the lyrics and composed the music for seventy anthems following that study. In addition, other religious compositions had been created by him. However, his life was the greatest testimony to the revelation that had come to him—the steady growth in grace and faith.

Dr. Brase kept a kind of informal spiritual diary for a few years during the 1930s. Some entries were copied from various authors; others were his own thoughts. A few citations from his papers written on single sheets indicate some aspects of his thinking.

> *December 22, 1930.* "Even weak faith is accompanied with peace and assurance. One feels that he is on the right road." Translated from a Swedish source.
>
> *January 13, 1931.* "We can rise above ourselves by identifying ourselves with a great cause or idea. Men are like flagpoles. Some are tall, some small. It makes little difference but it is all important that the colors they fly are right." Brase wrote beneath the quotation—"True." Harry Emerson Fosdick, radio sermon.
>
> *February 16, 1931.* "God screens us ever more from premature ideas. Our eyes are holden that we cannot see things that stare us in the face, until the hour arrives when the mind is ripened. Then we behold them." Ralph Waldo Emerson, *Spiritual Laws.*
>
> *August 1, 1932.* Psalm 139. "God is always near."
>
> *September 30, 1933.* "Lack of peace and a tormented conscience, longing for God, problems of making decisions—all these are proof that God seeks us, loves us and will help us. That is solace." Translated from Swedish.

Archbishop Erling Eidem was one of Hagbard Brase's favorite authors. The following, in translation, is one of Brase's citations from the writings of the well-known Swedish theologian:

> Strife and darkness are not evidence of God's wrath but rather that He has already established his good work in the soul....That I should shudder about myself, that I reach out in desperate anxiety toward one who can save me—that is not the path of damnation but it is the path on which God seeks me. These are the steps that lead to the land of life and promise. Here God most certainly dwells and this is the gate of heaven.

The sense of fellow feeling in the thought of Hagbard Brase is clear in the following statement which is a translation from an undesignated Swedish source: "God has patience with all of us so also we must have patience with one another, with other religious systems and religions, with other views, ways of living and weaknesses."

The role of Christian faith and thought is given a special and meaningful dimension in Dr. Brase's devotion to the study of Christianity and church music. His views are stated in the manuscript of a lecture on this topic. In it he sketches with broad strokes, figuratively speaking, the true origin of church music, its sources, historical influences and trends across the centuries.

Brase began his lecture by identifying the unique nature of Christianity:

> Christianity gave humanity a new soul. This new consciousness must express itself in new forms....But music could not develop until the new spirit of Christianity had begun its leavening work. It took many centuries before Europe was Christianized even in name and it was not until the twelfth century that music began to develop as an art.... The period from the twelfth century to the close of the sixteenth was one of extraordinary musical activity. That musical activity should settle around the church was natural at that time and in addition there were no concerts or concert halls. Musical talents were drawn to the church and worked almost exclusively toward enriching the liturgy.[4]

The influence of Martin Luther and the Reformers became an important factor in the development of church music:

> With the Reformation a new influence began to be felt in the church. For many centuries there had existed a kind of folksong, both sacred and secular. Martin Luther and his associates adapted many of these folksong melodies to the hymns which he and other Reformers wrote for the congregations. This was the beginning of the Lutheran chorales in their original compositions just as the composers before 1600 had used the tradition of the Catholic chants as the basis for their choral works.[5]

Music then entered into a process of growth and development. New styles were introduced and instrumental music attained greater promise. Secular influences were felt in sacred music:

> Church sources were not the only factors in promoting music. Instrumental music and opera had already become branches of music. Two styles of music, sacred and secular, developed side by side. But slowly the secular began to influence church music until the difference between sacred and secular music disappeared. However, one composer of church music, Johann Sebastian Bach, was able by his genius to use the combination of styles and still create works which we must recognize as true church music. After his death in 1750 the leadership of the church in the development of music comes to an end. But it had done its work well. Music has never lost the spiritual character it acquired during the centuries it was an art of the church.[6]

The influence of church music in the West was apparent in contrasting developments there with those in the Orient:

> We can speculate what music would have been now, if it had not been nourished by Christian thought. Nations like China and Japan with their old cultures have produced systems of music but they are not truly expressive of the soul and they seem incapable of development. The hu-

Dr. and Mrs. Hagbard Brase in later years.

man mind needed the deepening influence of Christianity before it could evolve a two tone language capable of experiencing its longings and aspirations.[7]

Hagbard Brase often expressed concern about the poor quality of church music in contrast with the great resources that were available:

> It is not a rash or startling remark when I say that much of what passes for music in the Christian church is entirely unworthy of the church. In schools, colleges and on the concert stage, wherever music is performed with a serious purpose, a high standard is maintained. In churches the emphasis is often on *how* the music is performed. We are fascinated by the technique of the performance, we admire the singing or playing, but we care little about the much more important question— What is performed? But this is the crux of the whole problem of church music in our day.
>
> The time will surely come when church music will receive its share of attention. The music literature of the Christian church is the richest and most profound of all branches of music. What is needed is a renaissance of church music. If that comes, the Christian church will again realize the grandeur and beauty of its own music.[8]

Hagbard Brase's seventy compositions published in the volume *Körsånger* (1901-02) provide interesting evidence of his view of one phase of church music. Lambert Dahlsten has interpreted this fine achievement as follows: "I am sure Hagbard Brase's *Körsånger* were designed to be liturgical rather than interpolated anthems. The texts were from the pericopes of the church year and with the nature of the music and the length of the compositions, one can only assume that they were meant to be introits, graduals, collects, etc., to be used for the specific day. This is part of Brase's sense of 'the fitness of things.'" Dahlsten further pointed out that the anthem as it is known today is a later British and American development and came into its present usage in the twentieth century.[9]

Dr. Brase was vitally interested in the Lutheran tradition of music since from earliest years to the end of his life he was closely identified with it. In another lecture, "Church Music and Its Development," he described the historical forces and trends with special reference to Martin Luther's influence:

> In changing from the Catholic Mass to the new form of service which became necessary as a result of the Reformation, Luther proceeded very cautiously. He kept the framework of the Mass, only omitting such prayers and ceremonies that were not in keeping with the new ideas. He was especially careful not to exclude the singing of the choir which continued to sing certain parts of the Mass even in Latin. For other parts he substituted congregational singing which became an increasingly important part of the service.[10]

Further emphasis in the lecture by Dr. Brase chronicled the changes

and developments in church music following the era of the Reformation. The influence of Bach was decisive:

> The Lutheran service has gone through many changes since Luther's
> time. In the seventeenth and part of the eighteenth centuries it was
> customary to sing a cantata before or after the sermon....This had pro-
> vided the opportunity for the greatest of all church music composers,
> Johann Sebastian Bach, to write a large number of cantatas. He wrote
> nearly 800 and about 200 have been preserved. The text of the cantata
> followed closely the Scriptural text for the Sunday when it was per-
> formed, and it consisted of choruses, recitatives, arias and one or more
> chorales. On certain festive days like Christmas and Easter, longer com-
> positions were performed.... Since Bach's time no new forms of good church
> music have developed.[11]

Hagbard Brase's Christian faith and thought and his interest in
church music enriched his personal life and provided abiding resources for his professional responsibilities. He lived from a great depth
of being and feeling. He could draw water, figuratively speaking, from
a deep well.

X.

Family and Friends

Family and friends in Sweden and America provided important resources in the life of Hagbard Brase and he, in turn, enriched the lives of those who had close kinship or friendship with him. The early death of *Komminister* Johannes Brase, his father, at the age of thirty-six, was an important factor in shaping his life. The result was that he lived in the world of the Jungner family from infant years until emigration to America at the age of twenty-three, except for some modification during the three years at Stockholm when he was a student at the Royal Conservatory of Music.

When Hagbard was only two years old, as has been described previously, his mother, sister Ingegerd and he lived for a brief time at Levene until the death of his grandfather, *Kyrkoherde* Johannes Jungner. They then moved to Skara where the principal influence, except for his mother, was *Rektor* Ernst Jungner of *Skara folkskolseminarium* (Elementary School Teacher Training College), his uncle. *Rektor* Jungner early recognized his nephew's talents and always encouraged him to work hard at his studies and music lessons in order to achieve high goals. Moreover, *Morbror* (uncle) Ernst did what he could to support Hagbard financially, although with a large family of his own, that help was modest. The uncle assisted Hagbard in securing loans during the Stockholm years. The Brases occasionally spent pleasant days at Uncle Ernst's summer home at Lundsbrunn near Skara.

Another important person in young Hagbard's life at this time was *Moster* Sofia, his mother's younger sister, who married *Komminister* Johan Linde. She moved to Skara after her husband's death in 1895 and lived there until her death in 1945. *Moster* Sofia assisted the Brases to the best of her ability, and was, of course, a great source of encouragement to Hagbard's mother in her continuing sorrow. *Moster* was proud of Hagbard's progress at *Skara läroverk* and later at the Royal Conservatory. Hagbard spoke with affection about his aunt. He also had good remembrances of Stina, a household worker who had served two generations of Jungners for sixty years. During the summer months Hagbard was occasionally a guest at the home of Jungner cousins. This was not always a pleasant time as revealed in his letters to his mother.

On the Brase side of the family only three aunts—Johanna, Brita and Maja-Stina—represented the paternal family. None of them married. Hagbard saw very little of Johanna and Brita, but he was intimately associated with Maja-Stina, whom he loved and esteemed. It was a sad day for Hagbard in early January 1898 when he said farewell to her before returning to his studies at Stockholm. She died shortly thereafter. Hagbard wrote later: "Maja-Stina had been a second mother to my sister and me and had taken care of my mother and our small household for more than fifteen years."[1]

Ingegerd, Hagbard's sister, was slightly more than a year older than her brother. As children they had a close relationship, sharing with their mother an uncertain life with a high degree of dependency on others. Ingegerd was a gifted student and made good marks in school. After graduating from the Skara Teacher's College, she taught school for a few years at Uddevala in *Bohus län* (a county in Sweden). In the early 1900s she became a member of Skara Teacher's College faculty where Uncle Ernst was *rektor*. The Principal of the College was Lisa Rydell, a fine person and an outstanding educator, who was Minna Hernwall's cousin. Ingegerd was always proud of her brother and his success in school and his music studies at Stockholm.

In June 1898 further sadness came to Ingegerd and Hagbard with the death of their mother, four months after the death of Aunt Maja-Stina. Their common sorrow brought brother and sister closer together. After Hagbard's emigration to America in the early autumn of 1900, Ingegerd and Hagbard met only during the summer of 1906 when Minna and he were in Sweden for a few months. Ingegerd was at Göteborg to wave goodby to her brother and his wife as they began the journey to America.

Ingegerd and Hjalmar Almfelt, Göteborg, a long-time friend of the Brase family, were married in 1907. They had two children—Oswald and Birgit. Hagbard's niece, Birgit, became a countess upon her marriage to Count Bengt Hamilton. Ingegerd's son, Harald Ryfors (Hagbard Brase's nephew) earned two advanced academic degrees from Uppsala University. He served as a *lektor* with the rank of senior teacher at Göteborg for several years, as *rektor* (principal or head-

Dr. and Mrs. Hagbard Brase celebrated their 40th wedding anniversary with the following family members. Left to right, front row: Katrina Bengtson Hock, (the dog is named "Toy,") and Barbara Lofgren Humphrey. Second row, seated: Edward Freeburg, Thorborg Russell, Hagbard Brase, Minna Brase, Olga Hernwall (sister-in-law), John Russell. Back row, standing: Ralph Russell, Sonja Bengtson Willey, Ralph Bengtson, Karin Freeburg, Arnold Freeburg, Ingrid Lofgren, Richard Lofgren, Gretchen Freeburg Hoyt, John Hoyt.

master) at Borås and as *rektor* of Göteborg's Higher School for Girls from 1957 to 1970. *Rektor* Ryfors has a fine record of service in educational, humanitarian and civic causes.

Hagbard had a close and loving relationship with his mother. Although she was frail in health from early years, she did her best in behalf of her son and daughter. Her limited economic resources caused her sorrow because she was not able to assist them as much as she wished to do. She maintained close contact with the Jungner relatives and friends and they assisted Hagbard in securing loans and other funds for his studies in Stockholm. She was a person of considerable courage and strong character; she transmitted to her children the will to achieve. She had the great satisfaction of knowing at the time of her death in 1898 that Ingegerd and Hagbard were making good progress in preparation for meaningful careers.

Hagbard Brase's family life in America provided a joyous contrast with the often somber experiences and circumstances of youthful years

Yngve Brase, who was not pictured at the 40th anniversary (previous page), is shown with his family in about 1952, in Denver. Left to right are: Patricia, Sonja, Stephen, Mattie, Paul, Yngve, and Kristen.

in Sweden. Minna and Hagbard's mutual love and esteem provided great resources for both of them. Their early years in America required many adjustments to the new social milieu. Minna was sometimes frustrated and unhappy over inability to maintain the high standard of living to which she had been accustomed in Sweden. She had great *hemlängtan* (longing for home) at the outset. It is quite possible that she was not fully comfortable with life in America until the later years. Hagbard made the observation, as noted previously, in his "Memoirs," written in 1945: "Mamma could not overcome the longing for Sweden for many years. Has she ever been reconciled to live here all her life?"[2]

Although Hagbard and Minna had this longing for the land of their birth, they entered into the life of the college and community with full devotion. They both worked hard. When Hagbard recalled his own capacity for sustained effort, he thought of Minna as he directed this question to their children: "What do you think of Mamma? I do not know of any more patient, heroic woman than she has been all these years."[3]

The birth of the five Brase children transformed the life of Hagbard and Minna, creating the great joy and concern that parents feel as they share the aspirations and problems of their growing children. Thorborg, the oldest, Karin, who was born in Sweden, and then, in order, Yngve, Sonja and Ingrid, constituted the family circle. An observer of the family is impressed with the strong feeling of family unity, the sharing of mutual interests, the tireless efforts of the parents to do what they could for the children, the cooperative response that was forthcoming and the rather strict paternal discipline in keeping with the European tradition.

The Brase children have good remembrances of their years together in the family circle. Thorborg recalls that meals were eaten under orderly conditions: "We stood behind our chairs until the youngest child said grace, then we were all seated. We were not allowed to leave the table until all had finished eating. I have happy memories of our meals when we were in teen years. We talked and argued about current affairs and Papa encouraged us to express our opinions. There was always a prayer before and after meals."[4]

Their father shared close participation with the children in daily activities. Thorborg has written: "Our father heard us say our prayers every evening when we were young. He went to each bed, sometimes we said them quickly and at other times he stayed to talk with us. I realize now what a patient man he was." Karin recalls that when the children were put to bed, and after he heard their prayers, he told them wonderful stories about Swedish kings and their courts. He also made up stories. A favorite was a story about the little flower that could not find a place to live until a fir tree promised to shelter her. The flower was the beautiful Linnea, named after Carl von Linné, famous Swedish botanist. Sonja also remembers those nightly prayers in both Swedish and English. In her generation the continuing story that her father made up was about Anna and Peter who lived in the forest. A good story teller, the father kept the children in suspense from night to night. When Sonja and her husband, Kenneth Willey, drove through the forests of Sweden during a visit to her father's home area in Västergötland, she thought about Anna and Peter and the stories from childhood days.[5]

Sonja and Ingrid, the younger daughters, always enjoyed a little ritual when they joined hands with their father, walking through the house and singing a Swedish song in rhymes about two men struggling through the snow. When all the stanzas had been sung, they danced around in a circle.[6]

Although the Brase children were not involved in sports with their father, who played neither golf nor tennis although the latter was popular with early time faculty members, he was a good swimmer and taught the children how to swim. Sonja looks back with pleasure to the summers when the children walked with their father to the sandpit, more than a mile from their home along the Smoky Hill River south of the Lindsborg city limits. There they received swimming lessons and enjoyed happy times together. Yngve was a fine athlete in high school and college football and basketball. His father attended these games.[7]

Hagbard Brase maintained close interest in the learning experiences of the children. Thorborg remembers well one summer when the subject was Swedish geography. She spent the mornings in her father's study reading about the *län* (county) of Sweden, the lakes and rivers. Periodically she would stand by his desk and recite the names of places and geographic divisions, or describe the route of the Göta Canal; or tell about the topography and history of the area where the Swedish relatives lived. Ingrid received early informal lessons in Swedish from her father by learning the word for items in a room or in the house as well as everyday expressions. She learned at an early age how to count in Swedish. When she was older her father helped her with themes in English. He was able to compress long, involved paragraphs into a few clear and concise sentences. The busy teacher and conductor enjoyed sharing time with the children.[8]

Dr. Brase was understandingly involved in the music studies of his children. The experiences were occasionally rather austere. Although Karin appreciated the time her father gave to her music lessons, the practice periods were not enjoyable. His standards and expectations were exacting and difficult to achieve. He worked with Ingrid in her attempt to master piano and viola lessons. His participation, especially in the former, involved intense concentration, and at times, "he helped with piano practice more than I wanted." Hagbard Brase did not encourage his children to perform in public. However, on one occasion Ingrid led group singing at a high school Father-Daughter banquet. Her father was pleased but surprised that she was able to do so.[9]

There were also happy times in the family related to music. Karin recounts with pleasure the many occasions when her father was at the piano with Thorborg, Yngve and she standing near him, singing Swedish songs out of two books, but especially from *Sjung med oss, mamma* (Sing With Us, Mamma). "How we loved those times," Karin later reported. On some Sunday evenings the group was larger as Margaret Sandzén joined them in the singing with Mrs. Sandzén at the piano and Birger Sandzén and Hagbard and Minna Brase also participating.[10]

Christmas was a gala time in the Swedish tradition. Mrs. Brase had been busy for weeks with "*Jul stök*" (Christmas bustle) and hiding packages in the closets. Dr. Brase decorated the Christmas tree during the morning of Christmas Eve, assisted by the children. The tree was provided with red candles and as the father lit the candles that evening, the family sat quietly in wonderment as they admired the lights. Yngve, while reminiscing about these times, pointed out the risk of fire from the burning wax candles attached to the dry Christmas tree. However, precautions had been taken since a tub full of water stood nearby in case of an emergency. The Christmas Eve festivities included at noon "*dopp i grytan*" (dunking bread in a delicious pot of soup). A week before Christmas the children began counting: "*dagen före dagen före dagen före doppare dagen*" (the day before the day before the day of dunking in the Christmas pot).[11]

After the gifts had been opened following dinner on Christmas Eve, the family formed a circle around the tree, dancing and singing "*Nu är det Jul igen*" (Now Christmas Is Here Again). Professor Oscar Thorsen and Professor G. A. Peterson were always present if they were in Lindsborg. The latter served as "*Jul Gubben*" (Santa Claus). C. V. Ostergren, M.D., Lindsborg Swedish physician, completed the Christmas guests. The gifts were small and inexpensive—a small doll, pencils, clothing and always a book. Karin still possesses a well-worn copy of Z. Topelius, *Läsning För Barn* (*Reading for Children*), which she received at Christmas 1909.[12]

At Christmas Eve dinner the Brases faithfully observed the custom of serving rice with a hidden almond. The unmarried person who received the almond was to be married the following year. During Christmas holidays there was always a bowl of nuts on the buffet. Anyone cracking a double almond had to find a member of the family and together entwine their arms and eat the almond as a wish was made. The one who remembered first to say *fillipino* to the other when they met next morning would receive his or her wish. This wish was never told.[13]

The happy events of Christmas Eve were followed next morning by the family's participation in the 6 a.m. Christmas Matins (*Julotta*) at the Bethany Church. There Dr. Brase played the organ as the congregation sang Johan Olof Wallin's famous hymn, "All Hail to Thee, O Blessed Morn" (*Var hälsad sjöna morgonstund*). He also led the choir in singing *Hosianna*! The thoughts of Minna and Hagbard quite likely were elsewhere at times as they recalled with deep feeling the festive *Julotta* services at Halmstad church and Skara cathedral. The Brase children sat in the Lindsborg church in a section that made it possible for them to see their father play the organ and lead the choir. This was another of the many occasions when they were proud of their father.[14]

The Brase family circle included thirteen grandchildren. The children were highly pleased with the attention that their father gave to their sons and daughters. When writing to Thorborg in 1947 he asked about his grandson: "How are you John? Your airplane is still grounded in the basement." Dr. Brase had enjoyed his grandson's interest in the model airplane and was looking forward to the time that John would return for another visit. When he acknowledged a gift that Thorborg had sent to him in January 1942, he expressed appreciation in an interesting manner: "I 'jike' it, as the twins would say." He was referring to Sonja and Patricia, twin daughters of Mattie and Yngve. The grandchildren remember how their grandfather entertained them by making funny faces and telling them interesting stories.[15]

Saturday evenings were special occasions for families in small towns during the early decades of this century. Thorborg recalls that her mother would shop at Hjerpe's, Sundstrom's and elsewhere while her father "babysat" the children on wide board planks at the Nickel-odeon, an early movie house where the Farmers State Bank is now located. Mrs. Brase gave the children some German chocolate as a special treat. While there is not much remembrance of the fast moving films, Thorborg describes these Saturday night shows as "a highlight of my life at that time." It is unlikely that Hagbard Brase gloried much in the entertainment but he enjoyed the company of his children and Mrs. Brase was free to do some essential shopping.[16]

The social life in Lindsborg was simple but interesting. A Swedish custom, Crayfish Day, was celebrated during August in the Smoky Valley. This was an exciting time for the children as reported by Thorborg: "We went with G. N. Malm, a friend of the family, to the Smoky Hill River dam near the mill to catch crayfish. We put them in gunnysacks and brought them a mile to the Malm residence. Mrs. Malm boiled the crayfish with dill in a wash tub. Papa, Mamma and other neighbors with their children came to Malm's backyard for a crayfish treat. As they ate and visited there were many stories, much laughter and Swedish songs.[17]

In the late spring and summer there were excursions in which the Brases joined other families and friends for picnics. The Spanish Steppes, northwest of Lindsborg, with Coronado Heights often the central point for the gatherings, and the Smoky Hill River on the south edge of Lindsborg, were common sites. Occasionally the destination was Horse Thief Canyon west of Marquette. This was an all day affair from dawn until darkness. The children remember especially one caravan of wagons and buggies, involving the John Welins, John Holmbergs, Birger Sandzéns and other families and unmarried teachers. Professor G. A. Peterson drove one wagon filled with old and young people, bouncing along the country roads and prairie trails to Horse Thief Canyon. Good food, lively conversation and stimulating hiking filled the day and on the homeward journey, in the gathering twilight, Swedish songs echoed across the hills and pastures. Many of these happy events are engraved, figuratively speaking, for life in the minds of the participants.[18]

There were many coffee parties in keeping with a well-established tradition in the old country as well as in Swedish America. Usually they were in the homes as friends and neighbors gathered for a pleasant time. The setting occasionally in spring and summer months was the college park, where Presser Hall is now located, or the open space between the evergreens in the Brase garden, or on the front porch of the Brase home. The women usually brought their needle work with them. The men came to enjoy briefly the delicious coffee and Swedish rolls and cakes.

A combination of tenderness and firmess characterized the Brase household, and the degree of the latter varied somewhat with the passing of the years. The older children lived more than the younger under strict discipline exercised largely by the father in the European tradition. There was more mellowness later, related perhaps to the growing adaptation to American life. The Brase children felt that differential in the context of their peer world, and the candor with which they express their remembrances is a tribute to the integrity which was a mark of identification of their home life.

The Brase children in Bethany Academy, which Thorborg and Karin attended, and in Lindsborg High School for the others, participated in the normal activities of their age groups. The same pattern prevailed at Bethany College. The four Brase daughters were members of Sigma Phi Omega sorority and Yngve was a member and officer of Pi Sigma Chi fraternity. The Brase daughters were attractive and popular. They had boy friends but there were limitations on dating that were more restrictive than those of their friends. A well established rule set 10 p.m. as the time limit for staying out. It is likely that Dr. Brase saw merit in the use of chaperones for young couples, although this was not required by him. The father was the principal factor in a fairly wide area of decision making. If he believed that the children should teach Sunday School or sing in the church choir, that would generally be the result. There would also be direct determination of vocational and professional career decisions. Karin wanted to be a nurse when she enrolled at Bethany College, but she was informed by Dean Oscar Lofgren that her father had signed her up for the course in Public School Music. This curriculum then became the one which she studied.[19]

The European view of Hagbard Brase was motivated by the paternalism of deep concern for the children and their welfare. Karin has pointed out that "Pop mellowed as the years went on. Sonja and Ingrid knew a different father from the one we older children knew. The grandchildren have fond memories of an affectionate and lenient grandfather. He was very proud of his grandchildren, a pride that his modesty never allowed him to show where his children were concerned. I am so pleased that Pop lived long enough and I matured enough to understand him and become close to him. We had many long talks about religion, history, politics, any subject that happened to come up."[20]

Thorborg has memories of her parents that go back to the westward passage across the Atlantic in 1906. She recalls how frightened she was in the cabin of the ship when the fog horn sounded as they approached the Boston harbor and how her father comforted her. She remembers also the ride in the cab at Boston, when she was scared by the "clop, clop" sound of the horses' hooves on the pavement and her father's skill in diverting her attention by saying, "Thorborg, look at the monkey," although there was no monkey. She cannot remember that her father ever spanked the children. She has written: "A hard look was enough for me when I needed discipline... 'Life with Father' did really revolve around our father. Papa and I had many good talks when I was growing up and I felt close to him. He was a kind hearted man who worried about the bills for his growing family and felt pressured by his ambitions and his inability to spend the time he wished on composing and developing other interests. I heard him say once that he had to choose between his garden and the a capella choir and he chose the choir."[21]

As the years passed Dr. Brase followed closely the activities of the children and their families. World War II made a great impact on them and on him. In a letter to Thorborg in August 1944 he described the situation: "Ingrid left for Miami Tuesday on the 3 a.m. train. Richard will meet her in Miami and they will take the train to Key West where he is a naval aviator. Ralph is studying in Chicago on an assignment with the navy. Sonja and Katrina are here. Your Ralph's army assignment has brought the two of you to Detroit. You know that Yngve is in Bridgeport, Connecticut, in his war related work. How you are spread over the country!" He concluded the letter by stating that "Mamma and Sonja are over at Berglunds. They have a meeting of the 'weavers.' I wonder how much they do."[22]

Hagbard and Minna Brase like all parents missed their children when they were absent and longed to see them. The father expressed their feelings in a letter to Thorborg in December 1945 when she was with Ralph who was assigned to Ft. Bragg in North Carolina: "You can hardly imagine how much it means to parents when they grow older to have their children near them."[23]

Saturday, September 29, 1951, was a memorable day for the Brase family. The parents' golden wedding anniversary was celebrated then to commemorate that day fifty years earlier when Hagbard and Minna were married in Lindsborg at the home of Birger and Frida Sandzén. There was great gratitude that all the Brase children and grandchildren had been able to share the gift of life from birth to this day. In keeping with the life style of the Brases, this was a personal day for members of the family, including Olga Hernwall, sister-in-law, and close personal friends, Oscar Thorsen and the Sandzéns. Telegrams and letters of good wishes came from Governor Edward F. Arn of Kansas and from a host of friends from near and far.

Hagbard Brase had many friends among colleagues at Bethany College, students, members of the oratorio society, residents of Lindsborg and people in a wide area. Mrs. Brase also had a large circle of friends, especially those who shared and admired her talent in weaving and Swedish needle work.

A special relationship of long standing prevailed in the close friendship of Hagbard Brase, Birger Sandzén and Oscar Thorsen. These three talented and dedicated men came from the same area of Västergötland. For more than half a century they taught, performed, conducted, composed music or painted with great distinction at Bethany College. Their unfailing loyalty and magnificent contribution to the college cannot be adequately described in words. The distinguished achievement of Bethany College in music and art would not have been possible to the same high degree without them. Their fellowship was mutually rewarding. In difficult times they could encourage (*uppmuntra*) one another. They had a common cultural and spiritual legacy with which they could identify and from which their lives were enriched. Acquaintanceship in Sweden developed into close and abiding friendship in Lindsborg.

Brase, Sandzén and Thorsen met almost daily at the college. They were often together with either the Brase or Sandzén families. Hagbard and Birger often visited in one or the other of their homes, when they intermittently used Swedish, French or German in order to maintain fluency in those languages. Other members of the family were not present on those occasions. When they went on walking excursions they sported canes, and in winter months they promenaded in carefully buttoned overcoats. The pace was not hurried; the bearing was stately. In family gatherings *Farbror* (Uncle) Hagbard and *Farbror* Birger were the common forms of personal and polite address by the children. The Hagbard Brase Room in beautiful Birger Sandzén Memorial Gallery on the Bethany College campus is an enduring testimonial to the long friendship of these two distinguished men. Margaret Sandzén Greenough's portrait of "Farbror Hagbard" is also an

Among the colleagues of Hagbard Brase are these Bethany College faculty members pictured in 1925, including the front row from the left: Dean Oscar Lofgren, Dr. Brase, Dean Emil O. Deere, President Ernst Pihlblad, (Oscar Thorsen is immediately behind Dr. Pihlblad), Birger Sandzen, Rev. O. L. Larson, and Prof. Linus Bohander.

appropriate identification of the close relationship of the Brase and Sandzén families across the years.

Oscar Thorsen, who came to Bethany at the turn of the century, was a close and dearly loved friend of the Brase family. The children called him *Farbror* Sen. He was always a part of the family circle on Christmas Eve. He would often drop in for a visit and was a welcome guest. In the early years when the Brases lived in the Almquist house, Oscar Thorsen lived with them. Thorsen and Brase each had a piano and they played late in the evening until Mrs. Brase made a rule that no one could play after 10:00 p.m. Thorsen was a talented pianist, a connoisseur of art, a man of high literary taste, a fine teacher, who provided generous hospitality to individuals and groups in his fascinating apartment above the Bethany Book Concern on North Main Street, the present location of Swedish Crafts.[24]

Another close friend was Professor G. A. (Gustavus Adolphus) Peterson, known at the college as "Swede Pete" in contrast with Professor Walter Peterson, "Greek Pete," and to the Brase children as

A view of the Brase garden in Lindsborg.

"*Fab Petson*," a shortened form of *Farbror* Peterson. Hagbard Brase and he met for the first time on the eastbound Atlantic crossing in 1906. When G. A. Peterson joined the Bethany faculty shortly thereafter, he lived for several years in the Brase household. The Brase children have many remembrances of this unique and interesting individual. They were especially pleased when he read Selma Lagerlöf's classic, *The Wonderful Journey of Nels Holgerson (Nils Holgersons underbara resa)*, which recounted the fascinating excursion of a boy around Sweden while riding on the back of a goose. As the interest of the children mounted, the reading might stop abruptly when "*Fab Petson*" said, "I must now grade my papers."[25]

G. N. Malm, Swedish-born designer-decorator, artist, author of the famous novel *Charli Johnson. Swedish-American (Charli Johnson. Svensk-Amerikan)* written in the so-called "mixed" Swedish-American language, oratorio society historian and college and community booster, was another of Brase's friends. They consulted often on a variety of issues and discussed many subjects. The Brase and Malm families also had close relations and shared in various social functions.

Members of the Bethany College faculty enjoyed their relationships with Brase. At the outset his closest association was not with the music teachers but with young liberal arts teachers like Ernst F. Pihlblad, Vivian Henmon, P. H. Pearson and others. When Dr. Pihlblad became president in 1904, this friendship continued and developed even more fully. Brase soon became acquainted with musicians Oscar Lofgren and Thure Jaderborg, who became life-long friends and colleagues, to be joined later by Arvid Wallin. The latter worked with Brase for many years as organist in performances of the oratorio society.

Closely associated with the Brases for several years was Agda Fred. They first met her on their visit to Sweden in 1906 as a seventeen year old girl who worked in the home of *Moster* Sofia at Skara. A native of that area, she was well liked by *Moster* Sofia and Hagbard and Minna Brase as she carried out the responsibility of taking care of Thorborg and Karin. Dr. Brase has written that the young lady had "America fever" and arrangements were made at the request of her parents so she could accompany the Brases on their return trip to America. Agda lived in the Brase home at the outset assisting Mrs. Brase with the children and other duties. She later worked elsewhere in Lindsborg until her marriage to Albin S. Nelson, a farmer who resided in the Fremont community west of Lindsborg. The Brase children enjoyed delightful visits at the farm home of Agda and Albin Nelson.[26]

Hagbard Brase had the good fortune to share life for more than half a century with Minna, his loving and loyal wife. The achievement of Dr. Brase is intimately associated with her willingness to go beyond the point of duty to support her husband, often at a sacrifice. She not only made a good home for him and their children but she entertained graciously many groups and individuals. Friday evening during "Messiah" Week, following the Bach concert, was devoted to entertaining guest soloists, principals in the festival events and others. Various groups and many individuals shared in the generous Brase hospitality from time to time. This was always a personal enterprise without college budgetary support.

Mrs. Brase was a talented person who contributed much to the life of the Lindsborg community across the years. Her great skill in handcrafts was widely recognized. She was a fine teacher and inspired those who came to her for help in weaving, hooking, needlepoint, bobbin lace, knitting, crocheting, China and tole painting. During World War I she was responsible for carrying out the Red Cross knitting program in the community and directed this enterprise in an effective and efficient manner. She was a member of the Bethany Lutheran Church, the Round Table Club, the Swedish Needlecraft Club, the Crafts Club and a charter member of the Bethany Teachers Wives, later known as the Bethany Dames.

Minna Brase was an avid and knowledgeable reader of biography, literature and history. She was quite likely the best patron of the college library and for many years she had the opportunity to read new books before they were accessioned. A well-informed and intelligent person, Mrs. Brase was an interesting conversationalist. She had been a good citizen of Lindsborg for more than seven decades at the time of her death June 2, 1972.

Photo views of Hagbard Brase
through the years in America.

XI.

The Years In Retrospect

People who knew Hagbard Brase have the clear image of a man of great dignity, walking slowly with measured steps, or on other occasions, standing erect, in control of himself and the situation whether before a chorus of hundreds of members or in conversation with a few people. A tall man, he was high waisted, of less than average weight perhaps, with a rather large frame. Quite bald in early middle years, he had a small mustache and goatee that turned white. His eyes were penetrating but friendly; he possessed a deep, resonant bass voice which produced a distinctive Swedish accent when he spoke English. His arms were long, hands large, the fingers narrowly tapered, created for a keyboard.

A natural courtesy characterized Hagbard Brase as a gentleman. He was a model of politeness. When walking and meeting a woman, he raised his hat, saying "Good morning," or "How-do-you-do," never "Hello." In manner of life and thought he reflected the best of Old World culture. Outwardly he seemed quite austere and reserved but he was actually a congenial and responsive person with a keen interest in people and their problems. He possessed an unusual capacity for gratitude—great appreciation even for small favors.

In conversation Hagbard Brase was a good listener, and when in agreement with his counterpart he often used the word, "Surely." His rate of speaking was slow and deliberate; he was thoughtful, there was never anything casual or cavalier in his speech although he had a good sense of humor. As a participant in conversation he was well informed both in questions and comments. He was a kind associate, a true friend, and an unforgettable character who generated esteem and respect.

Dedication to professional responsibilities and to his family occupied Dr. Brase fully but he managed to devote some time to personal interests and hobbies. He continued the physical exercise program associated with the name of Per Henrik Ling, famous Swedish gymnast, which he had learned in the land of his birth. A period was used each morning for this purpose. He often played solitaire at his desk at home for relaxation. On Sunday afternoons and during evenings on other days, whenever his schedule made it possible, he listened to radio concerts by the New York Philharmonic or other musical groups and to phonographic recordings, often with the aid of the orchestral or other score. Troubled by insomnia, he passed the hours reading history books or studying the scores of sonatas or symphonies. Dr. Brase was an avid reader; often Toy, Minna's dog, sat in his lap, as they both enjoyed mutual quiet contentment.[1]

Gardening was a hobby which Hagbard Brase thoroughly enjoyed. At *Skara läroverk* extensive studies in botany were required, including passing an examination in the Latin and Swedish names of hundreds of flowers and plants in the tradition of Linné, famous Swedish botanist. Love of nature was a great personal resource for the Lindsborg professor and musician. The importance of gardening was expressed in his autobiographical article in the series published by *Morgontidningen*, Göteborg in 1937: "My home and my garden are my hobbies. I do not always beat time with the baton; for a change I cut grass. When it becomes fatiguing to dig in music scores, I get pleasure from digging in the earth." He faithfully kept a garden diary with records of planting, growth progress, blooms, etc.[2]

A detailed description of Brase's garden was printed in *The Kansas City Star* in 1937 after a visit by the writer. On the sloping ground in the rear of the house were three terraces held by a retaining stone wall. The walls had been built by Dr. Brase. The terraces were landscaped and planted in shrubs, perennials and annuals in season. In the center of the second terrace was a pond where lilies bloomed and gold fish played. Overshadowing it was a great Babylonian weeping willow, its branches reflected in the still water of the pond. All around were flowers and shrubs. There was a quality about the entire arrangement which gave the impression that it was a natural garden. Included among the beautiful features of the Brase garden were two Chinaberry trees, probably the only trees of this kind in Lindsborg. They are a southern variety which grow luxuriously in the bayous of Louisiana. The berries are beautiful like amber China or glassbeads. June Currier Holmes observed in *The Lindsborg News-Record*: "It comes to mind that those trees in the Brase garden might reflect the sensitive taste for the beauty in nature as well as in music of Dr. Brase who planted them."[3]

Yngve, the middle child and only son of Minna and Hagbard Brase, feels that his father's interest in gardening, including growing vegetables, was important from several points of view. He observed that when his father used his surprising physical strength in spading the earth, lifting and placing heavy stones in the retaining wall of the terrace, and in trimming large trees, his outlook toward life was more exhuberant than previously. He became more vibrant and enthusiastic in the midst of physical labor. Yngve, who often worked side by side with his father, was not only impressed with his father's physical strength which he affirms was greater than his own, but he was so pleased that a fine fellowship and understanding developed between them. He had felt at times in the past that he really did not know his father and that they had very little in common. That was all changed now and for the future. Their relationships became more rewarding and happier than they had been previously.[4]

Astronomy was another of Hagbard Brase's interests and hobbies. He did much reading on the subject. The children were delighted when he described for them the beauty and mystery of the universe above them in the clear night sky.

As the years passed, the great career of Hagbard Brase was recognized by the award of special honors. On May 31, 1932, Augustana College and Theological Seminary, Rock Island, Illinois, awarded him the degree of Doctor of Music, *honoris causa*, for his distinguished service to music as a teacher, conductor, performer and composer.

The trip to Rock Island of Hagbard and Minna was made with Yngve in his 1928 Chrysler coupe. The journey from Lindsborg started out cheerfully, with an overnight stop at Marysville and a visit with Thorborg and her husband, Ralph Russell. When the Brases reached Iowa the next day they found that heavy spring rains had preceded them. The dirt roads were slick and difficult to navigate. On the downside slope of a steep hill it was impossible for Yngve to steer the car through a very hazardous and slippery section with the result that the car rested in the ditch without any injury to the passengers or damage to the vehicle. Yngve secured the generous aid of a farmer who hitched up two horses and pulled the car from the ditch. Dr. and Mrs. Brase were silent spectators as the action took place. When it was over, the former expressed his appreciation to the kind stranger and when he was told that the cost for this service would be fifty cents, the rescuer was pleased and surprised when Dr. Brase placed $2.00 in his hands.[5]

In October 1947 more than 200 persons assembled on the campus of Bethany College for a festive dinner occasion honoring Hagbard Brase. Gösta Oldenburg, Swedish Royal Consul General from Chi-

Less than a year before retiring as director, Hagbard with his wife Minna traveled to Kansas City by train in 1945 with the Bethany College Oratorio Society—to present "Messiah" excerpts in Municipal Auditorium as part of the Salvation Army 80th Anniversary observance.

cago, conferred upon Dr. Brase the title and insignia that created him a Knight of the Royal Order of Vasa on behalf of King Gustaf V of Sweden. This royal award, founded in the reign of Gustavus III in 1772, is conferred upon persons who have distinguished themselves in a variety of areas of service in the Swedish or Swedish-American context. This was an additional recognition of Hagbard's achievement in music. When Consul General Oldenburg presented Dr. Brase with this honor, the Bethany professor was greeted by a standing ovation.[6]

The Hagbard Brase Memorial Scholarship was established at Bethany College as a means of honoring Dr. Brase and assisting continuing generations of students.

Dr. Brase maintained a number of professional memberships throughout his career. Included were memberships in the America Guild of Organists, the New Bach Society of Leipzig, Gamma Mu chapter of the Sinfonia Fraternity of America and other organizations.

Hagbard Brase asked to be relieved of his position as director of the Bethany College Oratorio Society, as already indicated, following the 1946 festival season. He was Director Emeritus 1947-53. Brase conducted the a capella choir until the end of the academic year 1948. He continued to teach theory classes and organ full-time until shortly before his death in 1953. He was a part-time faculty member for a brief period.

When years and decades accumulate it is a common experience of those who are in that period of life to reflect upon early years and the passing of time. Hagbard Brase did just that in correspondence with Samuel Landtmanson, a boyhood friend from Skara years. In 1947 he wrote to Samuel: "The so-called American work tempo has slowed down somewhat for me and I can reflect on my years in America."[7]

As Brase reflected there was a combination of nostalgia, anxiety and hope. "My thoughts go back most of all to the years at Skara," he wrote. "Ingegerd sent me a copy of *Skaradjäknen* (The Skara College publication for former students) and I treasure the content and photographs." He remembered "the beautiful white and blue flowers, anemone (*vitsippor* and *blåsippor*) that bloomed as the snow disappeared, growing close to the earth, and the cowslips (*gullvivor*). I will never see them again." Hagbard was so appreciative of the New Year's greeting from Skara friends of long ago—Atti, Astrid, Esther, Tora, Ingeborg, Samuel and others. He also told his friend what he had expressed previously: "My wife and I certainly would have preferred to live in Sweden, especially after our visit there in 1906."[8]

As a sensitive person with a keen insight into the course of events, Brase had considerable anxiety about the future as he wrote to his friend Samuel Landtmanson: "The half century that I have lived in America has seen much progress in a technical sense but the character of people has undoubtedly worsened. Or are we perhaps dazzled by the machine age? Neither you nor I are too old to understand that we live in a foreboding era and in a world that is much more insecure than when we were children. Although you and I may escape the consequences, our children will be here for the storm that is in the process of developing."[9]

But there were hopes and promises for the future. He rejoiced in a fine family—Minna, five children and their spouses and grandchildren. Christmas 1951 had been especially festive. Minna and Hagbard had thoroughly enjoyed Christmas Eve and Christmas Day with Mattie and Yngve and their five children in Denver where the nearby snow-capped Rocky Mountains added natural splendor to the gala season. The traditions of the old country prevailed: "In our home we observe a Swedish Christmas, perhaps it should be described as a Västergötland Christmas. Our children and grandchildren don't think it's Christmas unless everything is like that."[10]

There were also other signs of joy and hope. In 1952 he wrote to his friend in Sweden: "Minna and I have our first great grandchild, born last year." They, too, belonged to the future through their children and their children's children.[11]

The generally good health of Dr. Brase is demonstrated by the fact that in more than three decades he missed only one oratorio performance, in 1945. In later years he felt at times somewhat less energetic than formerly and a leg condition that had impaired his walking temporarily on previous occasions was also somewhat troublesome. However, his condition did not interrupt faithful performance of college responsibilities.

Occasional fainting spells were experienced by Dr. Brase in later years. In 1947 his medical condition was diagnosed as pernicious anemia. He kept in close touch with Dr. William Holwerda, his Lindsborg physician. Life continued to be fairly normal although he told those closest to him that he did not feel as well as he would like to feel. He was not confined to bed but rested more than customarily. On the evening before Dr. Brase's death, Birger Sandzén, long-time friend and colleague, had a long and pleasant visit with him in the Brase home. This was the last of hundreds of visits across more than half a century.[12]

On Wednesday morning, March 18, 1953, Hagbard and Minna Brase awakened at the dawn of a new day. When Minna brought breakfast to the bedroom on the second floor of the home at 535 North Second Street in Lindsborg, in which they had lived since 1915, her husband had passed away quietly as the result of a heart attack.

When faculty members and students assembled for the daily chapel service that morning, they learned with deep sorrow about Dr. Brase's death. There was complete silence in the chapel as Reverend Emmet Eklund, college pastor, announced the passing of Bethany's great teacher and conductor. At the Brase home there was grief, but dignity and poise also, as Mrs. Brase talked quietly with Dr. William Holwerda, family physician, and Emory Lindquist, president of the college. Soon members of the family and friends came to face together a world in which Hagbard Brase was not present to share life directly with them.

A large congregation of friends and admirers of Hagbard Brase joined the family in impressive memorial services in the auditorium of Presser Hall on Sunday afternoon, March 22, 1953. There were many remembrances of Hagbard Brase coming unostentatiously to the podium, picking up the baton with quiet confidence, nodding to the concertmaster, after which were heard the strains of the "Overture" to Handel's *Messiah*. There were memories of those critical few minutes at each performance as the singers keyed up for No. 4, the first chorus selection, with eyes fastened upon the director, waiting for the signal to arise in unison, the playing of the first ten measures of the introduction by the orchestra, and then the auditorium resounding with the words of Isaiah set to music, "And the glory of the Lord shall be revealed." The chorus and the audience that March day 1953 had been participants in a great tradition with the beloved music master who would not raise his baton again.

The memorial service was conducted by friends and associates. The Reverend Ervin C. Malm, pastor of Bethany Lutheran Church in which Dr. Brase had been a member since 1900, preached the sermon. Dr. Emory Lindquist, president of Bethany College, spoke words of tribute; the Reverend Emmet Eklund, College pastor, and Dr. William Clark, a friend, also participated in the service.[13]

The oratorio society, with deep feeling, presented four selections. Some of the singers had been in the chorus continuously since that day in 1915 when Hagbard directed for the first time. A kindly spirit hovered over the audience in Presser Hall as the chorus sang Dr. Brase's favorites—"Surely He Hath Borne Our Griefs and Carried Our Sorrows" from *Messiah*, and from the *St. Matthew Passion*, "Our Sorrows Thou Art Bearing," "When Life Begins To Fail Me," "Here Yet A While." Rolf Espeseth conducted the chorus and orchestra, Lloyd Spear was concertmaster and Lambert Dahlsten was at the organ.

A large funeral cortege joined the family for graveside services at Elmwood Cemetery, a short distance east of Lindsborg. Casket bearers were colleagues at Bethany College. The burial rites were conducted by Pastor Malm in the liturgy of the Augustana Lutheran Church, an English translation of the Church of Sweden's order of service. On Saturday evenings the sound of the bells in the spire of the Bethany Church, which can be seen on the western horizon, reach this resting place and the chimes of the Messiah Lutheran Church bring the message of Christian hymnody, including familiar hymns from the old homeland across the Atlantic Ocean.

Hagbard Brase began his earthly pilgrimage at Råda in Västergötland and the end was at Lindsborg in the Smoky Valley of Central Kansas. It was a journey that was lived fully and victoriously.

END NOTES

I. The Early Years in Sweden

1. Hagbard Brase, "Släktregister," p. 8; Hagbard Brase, "Memoirs of Hagbard Brase," p. 2. Referred to hereafter as "Memoirs of Hagbard Brase." A manuscript, 35 pp. single-spaced, typed.
2. L. A. Cederbom and C. O. Friberg, *Skara stifts herdaminne 1850–1930* (Stockholm, 1928), I, 119-21; Brase, "Släktregister," p. 6.
3. *Skara stifts herdaminne, I, 501-02.*
4. *Ibid.*
5. *Ibid.*, I, 501.
6. *Ibid.*
7. Lydia Brase to Fru Johan Jungner, Råda, September 13, 1878.
8. *Skara stifts herdaminne*, I, 502.
9. "Memoirs of Hagbard Brase," p. 2–3.
10. *Ibid.*, p. 3.
11. *Ibid.*, p. 4.
12. *Ibid.*, pp. 4, 8.
13. Gustaf Holmstedt, *Skara läroverk 1641–1941. Festskrift.* (Stockholm, 1941), "Företal" and pp. 12–13.
14. "Memoirs of Hagbard Brase," p. 5.
15. *Ibid.*, p. 9.
16. "Memoirs of Hagbard Brase," p. 5; Holmstedt, *Skara* läroverk, pp. 147, 129, 119, 123, 122.
17. "Utdrag ur afgångsbetyg från Skara högre allm. läroverk, Skara den 29 augusti 1895;" Sofia Linde to Hagbard Brase, Skara, June 6, 1895.
18. "Memoirs of Hagbard Brase," p. 6. The song was composed by Adolf Fredrik Lindblad (1801-79).
19. *Ibid.*, p. 8.
20. *Ibid.*, p. 7.
21. *Ibid.*
22. *Ibid.*, p. 8.
23. *Ibid.*, p. 5.
24. *Ibid.*, p. 11.
25. Otallo Morales and Tobias Norlund, *Kungl. musikaliska akademien 1771– 1921* (Stockholm, 1921), p. 132. The Royal Conservatory of Music was known in Brase's time as *Kongl. musik-konservatorium.* In 1905 the spelling was changed from *Kongl.* to *Kungl. musik-konservatorium.* It was reorganized and renamed the *Kungl. musikhögskolan* (Royal Col-

lege of Music) in 1940. In 1971 the Royal College of Music was separated from the Royal Swedish Academy of Music and became known as the *Musikskolan i Stockholm* (Stockholm Music College). Similarly state-operated music colleges were founded in Göteborg and Malmö. The present address of the *Musikskolan* is Valhallavägen 103–109. Booklet, *The Royal Swedish Academy of Music* (Stockholm, 1983), 27 pp; correspondence, Karin Stenfors with Emory Lindquist, Stockholm, November 4 and December 13, 1983.

26. "Memoirs of Hagbard Brase," p. 11.

II. Music Studies in Stockholm

1. "Memoirs of Hagbard Brase," p. 11.
2. "Memoirs of Hagbard Brase," p. 16; "Kurser," *Kongl. musikaliska akademiens läroverksstyrelse 1888*, pp. 1–3.
3. "Memoirs of Hagbard Brase," p. 17; "Kurser" pp. 4–7.
4. "Memoirs of Hagbard Brase," pp. 16–18; "Kurser," pp. 7–8.
5. "Memoirs of Hagbard Brase," p. 17; "Kurser," p. 7.
6. Hagbard Brase, "Examensbetyg från *Kongl. musikkonservatorium*, April 24, 1899," p. 13.
7. "Memoirs of Hagbard Brase," pp. 22–23.
8. *Ibid.*
9. Hagbard Brase, "Examensbetyg från *Kongl. musikkonservatorium*, May 31, 1900," (two lists of *betyg*).
10. "Memoirs of Hagbard Brase," p. 19 (and collection of programs).
11. *Ibid.*, p. 15.
12. *Ibid.*, p. 18.
13. Lydia Brase to Hagbard Brase, Skara, May 18, 1898; "Memoirs of Hagbard Brase," pp. 15–16.
14. Lydia Brase to Hagbard Brase, Skara, two letters, one undated and the other September 23, 1897.
15. Brita Brase to Hagbard Brase, Bitterna, November 7, 1897.
16. "Memoirs of Hagbard Brase," p. 25.

III. An Interlude

1. "Memoirs of Hagbard Brase," p. 20.
2. Hagbard Brase, "Släktregister," pp. 18–19.
3. "Memoirs of Hagbard Brase," p. 20.
4. Hagbard Brase, "Dagbok," June 20, 1899.
5. *Ibid.*, June 23–25, 1899.
6. *Ibid.*, July 4, 1899.
7. *Ibid.*, July 4–6, 1899.
8. *Ibid.*, July 12, 1899.
9. *Ibid.*, July 15, 1899.
10. *Ibid.*, July 18, 1899.

11. *Ibid.*, July 19, 1899.
12. *Ibid.*, July 21, 1899.

                    IV. Emigration and Early Years in America

1. "Memoirs of Hagbard Brase," p. 25.
2. "Självbiografiska artikelserie, 'Hagbard Brase,'" *Morgontidningen*, Göteborg, October 2, 1937.
3. "Memoirs of Hagbard Brase," p. 26.
4. *Ibid.*
5. *Ibid.*
6. *Ibid.*
7. *Ibid.*
8. Hagbard Brase to Minna Hernwall, Lindsborg, Kansas, November 2, 1900.
9. *Ibid.*
10. *Ibid.*
11. *Ibid.*
12. "Memoirs of Hagbard Brase," p. 27.
13. Background information about the history of Bethany College is found in Emory Lindquist, *Bethany in Kansas. The History of a College* (Lindsborg, Kansas, 1975), pp. 1-22.
14. *The Lindsborg News*, November 9, 1900; "Memoirs of Hagbard Brase," pp. 27–28.
15. *Bethany College Catalogue, 1900-01*; brochure, "The Messiah" at Lindsborg, 1901.
16. Hagbard Brase, "Dagbok," July 16, 1899.
17. *Ibid.*
18. "Memoirs of Hagbard Brase," p. 29.
19. "Memoirs of Hagbard Brase," p. 29; Birger Sandzén to Gustaf Sandzén, Lindsborg, Kansas, October 6, 1901.
20. "Memoirs of Hagbard Brase," p. 30.
21. *Ibid.*
22. *The Lindsborg News*, November 16, 1901.
23. *Ibid.*
24. *Ibid.*
25. Quoted in Lindquist, *Bethany In Kansas*, p. 35.
26. "Memoirs of Hagbard Brase," p. 31.
27. *Bethany College Catalogue, 1900-01*. p 68; *1903-04*. pp. 62–63; *1904-05*. pp. 64-66.
28. *Ibid.*, *1903-04*. p. 61.
29. "Memoirs of Hagbard Brase," p. 32.
30. *Augustana* (Rock Island, Illinois). October 3, 1901.
31. *Augustana*, November 7, 1901; "Memoirs of Hagbard Brase," p. 32.
32. "Memoirs of Hagbard Brase," p. 30.
33. *Ibid.*, p. 31.
34. *Ibid.*

35. *Ibid.*, pp. 31–32.
36. *Ibid.*, p. 32.

V.   To Sweden and Lindsborg Again

1. "Memoirs of Hagbard Brase," p. 32, *Yale Alumni Weekly* quoted in the *Bethany Messenger*, November 9, 1902; Interview of Sonja Willey with Emory Lindquist, October 2 and October 21, 1982.
2. "Memoirs of Hagbard Brase," p. 32.
3. "Memoirs of Hagbard Brase," p. 33; "Ships List of *S. S. Caledonia.*"
4. "Memoirs of Hagbard Brase," p. 33.
5. *Ibid.*
6. Mrs. Birger Sandzén to Mrs. Erik Leksell, Asklanda, Sweden, July 10, 1905; "Memoirs of Hagbard Brase," p. 33.
7. "Memoirs of Hagbard Brase," p. 33.
8. *S. S. Republic* passenger list, September 26, 1906; "Memoirs of Hagbard Brase," p. 33.
9. *The Lindsborg Record*, October 12, 1906.
10. "Memoirs of Hagbard Brase," p. 34.
11. *Ibid.*
12. *Bethany College Catalogue, 1909-10*, pp. 77–78; pp. 113–117.
13. Hagbard Brase, "Introduction," *Valda koraler* (Rock Island, Illinois, 1910).
14. *The Bethany Messenger*, January 30, 1908; May 4, 1912.

VI.   Hagbard Brase and the Lindsborg "Messiah" Tradition

1. *Kansas konferensens referat 1915*, pp. 144–45.
2. *The Lindsborg Record*, April 2, 1915.
3. *Lindsborgs-Posten*, March 31, 1915.
4. *The Kansas City Star*, April 6, 1915.
5. *Ibid.*, April 17, 1916. Brase attended a performance of *Messiah* by the Apollo Musical Club of Chicago in December 1915.
6. *The Lindsborg News-Record*, April 6, 1917.
7. *The Kansas City Star*, May 6, 1918.
8. *The Lindsborg News-Record*, May 13, 1918; *Omaha Bee News*, March 24, 1939; *The Kansas City Star*, May 14, 1918.
9. Edith Johnson, *The Daily Oklahoman*, February 8, 1922.
10. *The Oklahoma Times* quoted in *The Lindsborg News-Record*, March 31, 1922.
11. *The Kansas City Star*, November 19, 1922.
12. *Ibid.*, November 20, 1922.
13. *The New York Times*, February 4, 1923.
14. *Ibid.*
15. *The Lindsborg News-Record*, April 12, 1928; Jaci Black and Emory Lindquist, "The Lindsborg 'Messiah' Chorus," a manuscript study of membership in the oratorio society.

16. *The Lindsborg News-Record*, April 12, 1928.
17. *Lindsborgs-Posten*, April 4, 1928, *The Lindsborg News-Record*, April 12, 1928.
18. *The Lindsborg News-Record*, March 26, 1929.
19. *The Kansas City Journal-Post*, December 15, 1929.
20. *The Kansas City Star*, December 15, 1929.
21. *The Kansas City Times*, April 17, 1933.
22. *The Kansas City Star*, April 14, 1935.
23. *Ibid.*
24. *The Bethany Messenger*, April 1920.
25. *The Lindsborg News-Record*, April 25, 1935.
26. *The Kansas City Star*, April 18, 1938; *Musical Courier*, May 10, 1938.
27. *The Wichita Beacon*, April 16, 1934.
28. *The Lindsborg News-Record*, April 10, 1941.
29. Blanche Lederman, *Musical America*, April 25, 1941.
30. *The McPherson Daily Republican*, March 17, 1942; *The Kansas City Times*, March 30, 1942.
31. *The Lindsborg News-Record*, April 21, 1943.
32. *The Salina Journal*, April 11, 1944.
33. *The St. Louis Post-Dispatch*, April 9, 1944; *The Salina Journal*, April 11, 1944.
34. *The Salina Journal*, April 11, 1944.
35. *The Lindsborg News-Record*, November 15, 22, 1945.
36. *Ibid.*; March 22, 1945.
37. Minnie K. Powell, *The Kansas City Star*, September 1, 1946.
38. Howard W. Turtle, "Kansas Festival," *The New York Times*, March 26, 1939.
39. *The Kansas City Times*, March 22, 1948.
40. *Ibid.*
41. Interview of Sonja Willey with Emory Lindquist, October 21, 1982.

VII. Singing the "St. Matthew Passion" and Other Sacred Song

1. Interview of Ingrid Brase Lofgren with Emory Lindquist, March 16, 1982.
2. *The Kansas City Star* reprinted in *The Bethany Messenger*, April 24, 1920.
3. *Ibid.*
4. *The Bethany Messenger*, January 31, 1920.
5. Hagbard Brase, Lecture, "Notes on *The Passion of Our Lord According to St. Matthew* by Johann Sebastian Bach," 5 pp.
6. *The Lindsborg News-Record*, November 26, 1925.
7. *Ibid.*
8. *Ibid.*, November 21, 1926.
9. *Ibid.*, April 4, 1929.
10. Jaci Black and Emory Lindquist, "The Lindsborg 'Messiah' Chorus," a manuscript.
11. *The Kansas City Star*, April 9, 1933.
12. Guy Criss Simpson, "Doing the 'St. Matthew Passion,'" *The American*

Organist 20 (September 1937), 313.
13. *The Kansas City Times*, April 16, 1938.
14. *The Lindsborg News-Record*, April 17, 1941.
15. Program, *The St. Matthew Passion*, presented by the Bethany College Oratorio Society, 1943.
16. *The Lindsborg News-Record*, May 28, 1936.
17. *Ibid.*
18. *The Wichita Eagle*, May 8, 1938.
19. James William Finley to Hagbard Brase, Princeton, New Jersey, May 19, 1938; *The Wichita Eagle*, May 8, 1938.
20. Louis H. Diercks to Hagbard Brase, Columbus, Ohio, May, 1938.
21. *The Reporter-Herald*, Loveland, Colorado, April 9, 1940.
22. *The Kansas City Star*, March 24, 1951.
23. *The Lindsborg News-Record*, January 6, 1944.
24. Memorial Service in Honor of Hagbard Brase, Bethany Lutheran Church, April 4, 1954, Order of Service.

VIII.   Conducting, Teaching and Composing

1. Hagbard Brase, "Training An Oratorio Chorus," pp. 1–2. A manuscript, 12 pp.
2. *Ibid.*, pp. 2–3.
3. *Ibid.*, pp. 3–4.
4. *Ibid.*, pp. 4–5.
5. *Ibid.*, pp. 5–6.
6. *Ibid.*, pp. 6–7.
7. *Ibid.*, pp. 7–8.
8. *Ibid.*, p. 8.
9. *Ibid.*, pp. 8–10.
10. *Ibid.*, p. 10.
11. *Ibid.*, pp. 11–12.
12. Lambert Dahlsten in "Remembrances of Hagbard Brase by Former Students," pp. 13–14; Lloyd Spear, p. 39. This is a manuscript collection of experiences and views of former students compiled in 1982. Hereafter identified as "Remembrances."
13. Ralph Harrel in "Remembrances," p. 23.
14. *Ibid.*, p. 24.
15. Elmore Carlson in "Remembrances," pp. 7–8.
16. Lambert Dahlsten in "Remembrances," p. 19.
17. Jessie Ash Arndt, *The Christian Science Monitor*, March 8, 1944.
18. *Ibid.*
19. Rosalie Carlson Nelson in "Remembrances," p. 37.
20. Albertha Sundstrom in "Remembrances," p. 46; Nadine Burwell Berggren, p. 51; Allison Chandler, p. 9.
21. Chancellor Frank Strong to Hagbard Brase, Lawrence, Kansas, June 15, 1915; "Minutes of the Meeting of the Board of Directors of Bethany College, July 13, 1915"; Ronald Lofgren, "The Life of Hagbard Brase," pp.

6–7. An interesting and informative description of Dr. Brase by a grandson.

22. Hagbard Brase, Lecture, "Christianity and Music," p. 6.

23. *Ibid.*, pp. 6–9.

24. Nelouise Hodges Stapp in "Remembrances," p. 41; Lloyd Spear, p. 40.

25. Hagbard Brase to Doris Ylander, Lindsborg, Kansas, October 7, 1950; Doris Ylander to Emory Lindquist, Wichita, Kansas, March 6, 1983.

26. Eloise Perry Dale and Della Brown Crawford to Hagbard Brase, A Capella Choir Reunion, March 1951; Nadine Berggren in "Remembrances," p. 5.

27. Lois Wells in "Remembrances," p. 49.

28. Ralph Harrel in "Remembrances," p. 23.

29. Roberta Pruitt Martin in "Remembrances," p. 49.

30. Lambert Dahlsten in "Remembrances," p. 18; Nelouise Stapp, p. 41.

31. Joanne Johnson in "Remembrances," p. 27–28.

32. Rosalie Carlson Nelson in "Remembrances," p. 37.

33. Norman Johnson to Hagbard Brase, Grand Rapids, Michigan, A Capella Choir Reunion, March 1951; Nadine Hagstrand Bohning in "Remembrances," p. 6.

34. Helemae Pearce Johnson in "Remembrances," p. 25.

35. Nelouise Hodges Stapp in "Remembrances," p. 42; Maridene Newell Lundstrom, p. 29.

36. Helenmae Pearce Johnson in "Remembrances," p. 25; Joanne Johnson, p. 28.

37. Margaret Bloomquist in "Remembrances," p. 4.

38. Carol N. Anderson in "Remembrances," p. 2.

39. "Minutes of the Meeting of the Board of Directors of Bethany College, July 13, 1915;" Ronald Lofgren "The Life of Hagbard Brase," pp. 8–9.

40. "Minutes of the Meetings of the Board of Directors of Bethany College"—salary data for the years indicated.

41. *The Music News*, November 5, 1915.

42. *The Bethany Messenger*, April 5, 1924.

43. *Ibid.*, April 26, 1924.

44. Lambert Dahlsten in "Remembrances," p. 16–17.

45. Roberta Pruitt Martin in "Remembrances," pp. 35–36.

IX. Christian Thought, Faith and Music

1. "Memoirs of Hagbard Brase," pp. 24–25.

2. For background information about Olof Olsson please see Emory Lindquist, *Vision for a Valley. Olof Olsson and the Early History of Lindsborg* (Rock Island, Illinois, 1970), pp. 27–52.

3. Hagbard Brase, manuscript copies untitled but dated August 22, 1930, and September 30, 1933.

4. Hagbard Brase, "Christianity and Music," pp. 2–3. Manuscript copy, 11 pp.

5. *Ibid.*, p. 4.

6. *Ibid.*, pp. 4–5.
7. *Ibid.*, pp. 5–6.
8. *Ibid.*, pp. 10–11.
9. Lambert Dahlsten in "Remembrances of Hagbard Brase," p. 22. (See pp. 37–38 of this volume for a description of the *Körsanger*.)
10. Hagbard Brase, "Church Music and Its Development," p. 7. Manuscript item, 22 pp.
11. *Ibid.*, pp. 7–8.

X.   Family and Friends

1. "Memoirs of Hagbard Brase," pp. 19–20.
2. *Ibid.*, p. 34.
3. *Ibid.*, p. 30.
4. Thorborg Brase Russell in "Memories of Our Father," p. 20. Manuscript material prepared by the Brase children in 1982.
5. Thorborg Russell to Emory Lindquist, Mankato, Kansas, April 30, 1982; Karin Brase Freeburg in "Memories of Our Father," p. 11; Sonja Brase Willey, p. 16.
6. Sonja Willey in "Memories of Our Father," p. 17; Ingrid Brase Lofgren, p. 1.
7. Sonja Willey in "Memories of Our Father," p. 17.
8. Thorborg Russell in "Memories of Our Father," p. 20; Ingrid Lofgren, pp. 7, 9.
9. Ingrid Lofgren in "Memories of Our Father," p. 12; Karin Freeburg, p. 12.
10. Karin Freeburg in "Memories of Our Father," p. 15.
11. Yngve Brase, tape recording, Denver, Colorado, October 1982; Karin Freeburg in "Memories of Our Father," p. 13.
12. Thorborg Russell in "Memories of Our Father," pp. 20–21; Karin Freeburg, p. 12.
13. Sonja Willey in "Memories of Our Father," pp. 17–18; Thorborg Russell, pp. 20–21; Karin Freeburg, pp. 12–13.
14. Thorborg Russell in "Memories of Our Father," p. 21.
15. Hagbard Brase to Thorborg Russell, Lindsborg, Kansas, October 12, 1947; Sonja Willey in "Memories of Our Father," p. 16.
16. Thorborg Russell in "Memories of Our Father," p. 20.
17. *Ibid.*, p. 21.
18. *Ibid.*, pp. 21–22.
19. Karin Freeburg in "Memories of Our Father, pp. 12–13.
20. *Ibid.*, pp. 14–15.
21. Thorborg Russell in "Memories of Our Father," p. 22.
22. Hagbard Brase to Thorborg Russell, Lindsborg, Kansas, August 9, 1944. Identification of names: Richard Lofgren, Ingrid's husband; Ralph Bengtson, Sonja's husband; Ralph Russell, Thorborg's husband.
23. *Ibid.*, December 31, 1945.
24. Thorborg Russell in "Memories of Our Father," p. 19.

25. *Ibid.*
26. "Memoirs of Hagbard Brase," p. 33; Interview of Carl A. Nelson with Emory Lindquist, Wichita, Kansas, June 20, 1982.

XI. The Years in Retrospect

1. Sonja Willey in "Memories of Our Father," p. 16; Ingrid Lofgren, p. 5.
2. "Självbiografiska artikelserie, 'Hagbard Brase,'" *Morgontidningen* (Göteborg), October 2, 1937.
3. *The Kansas City Star*, January 17, 1937; "Hagbard Brase Scrap Book," No. 1.
4. Yngve Brase, tape recording, Denver, Colorado, October 1982.
5. *Ibid.*
6. *The Lindsborg News-Record*, October 9, 1947.
7. Hagbard Brase to Samuel Landtmanson, Lindsborg, Kansas, July 20, 1947.
8. *Ibid.*, December 22, 1949.
9. *Ibid.*
10. *Ibid.*, January 13, 1952.
11. *Ibid.*
12. *Ibid.*, July 20, 1947.
13. *The Lindsborg News-Record*, March 19, 1953; *The Kansas Conference Lutheran* (Lindsborg, Kansas), April 1953; Order of Memorial Service in Presser Hall, March 22, 1953.

SELECTED BIBLIOGRAPHY

UNPUBLISHED SOURCES

Brase, Hagbard. "Bach and Handel." A lecture.

────── "Christianity and Music." A lecture.

────── "Church Music and Its Development." A lecture.

────── "Collection of Religious Observations."

────── "Correspondence, 1890–1953."

────── "*Dagbok,* June 23–July 21, 1899."

────── "Memoirs." 1945

────── "The Passion of Our Lord According to St. Matthew." A lecture.

────── "A Religious Experience, August 22, 1930."

────── "*Släktregister.*"

────── "Some Observations About the Music of the Morning Worship Service." A lecture.

────── "The Text and Music of *Niebelungen Ring.*" A lecture.

────── "Training an Oratorio Chorus." A lecture.

Black, Jaci, and Lindquist, Emory, "The Lindsborg 'Messiah' Chorus. A Study of the Membership." 1975.

Correspondence. Miscellaneous. Brase, Brita; Brase, Lydia; Brase, Mrs. Minna Hernwall; Crawford, Della Brown; Dierks, Louis H.; Finley, James William; Dale, Eloise Perry; Johnson, Norman; Landtmanson, Samuel; Linde, Sofia; Russel, Thorborg Brase; Ryfors, Harald; Sandzén, Birger; Sandzén, Mrs. Birger; Sandzén, Gustaf; Sandzén, Johan; Stenfors, Karin; Strong, Frank; Swensson, Carl A.; Ylander, Doris.

"Examens betyg från Kongl. musikaliska konservatorium, April 24, 1899, and May 31, 1900."

Lofgren, Ronald., "The Life of Hagbard Brase." 1975.

"Memories of Our Father, Hagbard Brase." 1982. Russell, Thorborg; Freeburg, Karin; Brase, Yngve; Willey, Sonja; Lofgren, Ingrid.

"Remembrances of Hagbard Brase," 1982. Unpublished statements by eighteen former students.

"Utdrag ur afgångsbetyg från Skara högre allm. läroverk." 1895.

"Minutes of the Meetings of the Faculty of Bethany College, 1900–1953."

Minutes of the Board of Directors of Bethany College, 1900–1953."

PRINTED SOURCES

"America's Oberammergau on the Plains of Kansas." *New York Times*, February 4, 1923

Arndt, Jessie Ash. "The 'Messiah' at Lindsborg." *Christian Science Monitor*, Boston, March 18, 1944.

Bailey, Herbert M. " 'Messiah' Festival at Lindsborg, Kansas." *The Music News*, May 1915.

Behymer, F. A. "Oberammergau of the Plains." *St. Louis Post Dispatch*, April 9, 1944

Bethany College Bulletin, December 20, 1915. Special issue with important articles about the oratorio society.

Bethany College Catalogue. 1900-53.

Bethany Daisy. 1908-53.

Bethany Messenger. 1907-53.

Brase, Hagbard. *Körsånger för sopran, alt, tenor och bas. Med text för förste nya årgångers evangelier*. Rock Island: Augustana Book Concern, 1903.

———. "Några tankar angående kyrkosången inom Agustana Synoden," *Augustana. Tidning för den Svenska lutherska kyrkan i Amerika*. August 17, 1904.

———. "Musiken vid våra svensk-amerikanska läroverk" in *Prärieblomman kalender för 1908*. Rock Island: Augustana Book Concern, 1908. pp. 73–86.

———. *Valda koraler i gammalrytmisk form*. Rock Island: Augustana Book Concern, 1910.

———. "Den lutherska församlingenssånger före och nu." *Lindsborgs-Posten*, July 15 and 22, 1910.

———. "Konst och musik i Lindsborg." In Bergin, Alfred. *Lindsborg efter femtio år*. Lindsborg: Bethany Lutheran Church, 1919. Also in Bergin, Alfred.

The Smoky Valley in After Years. Translated by Ruth Billdt and edited by Elisabeth Jaderborg. Lindsborg: *Lindsborg News Record*, 1969.

———. "Självbiografiska artikelserie." *Morgontidningen*, Göteborg, October 2, 1937.

———. Hagbard Brase Scrapbooks. 3 volumes.

Cederbom, L. A. and Friberg, C. O. *Skara stifts herdaminne 1850–1930*. Stockholm: Svenska kyrkans diakonistyrelses bokförlag, 1938.

"Death Comes Suddenly to Dr. Brase." *Lindsborg News Record*, March 19, 1953.

"Directs 'Messiah' Chorus from 1915 -1945." *Lindsborg News-Record*, March 22, 1945.

"Dr. Brase Is Knighted by Swedish Government." *Lindsborg News-Record*, October 9, 1947.

Holmstedt, Gustaf. *Skara läroverk 1641–1941. Festskrift*. Stockholm: P. A. Norstedt & Söner, 1941.

Katalog över Skara högre allmänna läroverk 1899-1894. Skara.

Kurser. Kongl. musikaliska akademiens läroverksstyrelse. 1888. Stockholm.

Lederman, Blanche. "Lindsborg Has 60th Annual 'Messiah' Festival." *Musical America* 61: (April 25, 1941)

Levenebygden. Levene, Long, Slädene, Sparlösa. Vara: Levene hembygdsförening, 1976.

Lindquist, Emory. *Smoky Valley People. A History of Lindsborg*. Lindsborg: Bethany College: 1953.

———. *Vision for a Valley. Olof Olsson and the Early History of Lindsborg*. Rock Island: Augustana Historical Society, 1970.

———. *Bethany In Kansas. The History of a College*. Lindsborg: Bethany College, 1975.

The Lindsborg Record, 1900-12.

The Lindsborg News, 1900-12.

The Lindsborg News-Record, 1912-53.

Lindsborgs-Posten, 1898-1930.

"Lindsborg Hears Annual Festival." *Musical America*, May 10, 1938.

"Lindsborg, Kansas, 'Messiah' Festival." *Musical Courrier*, April 13, 1916.

"Lindsborg's 'Messiah'." *Newsweek*, April 3, 1939.

Malm, G. N. "Messias sången på prärien." *Korsbaneret kristlig kalender för 1905.* Pp. 119-50.

" 'Messiah' Week at Lindsborg, Kansas." *New York Times,* February 4, 1923.

"The 'Messiah' 1882–1907." *Quarter Centenniel Anniversary. 1907.* Lindsborg, Kansas.

Morales, Olallo, and Norlind, Tobias. *Kungl. musikaliska akademien 1771– 1921.* Stockholm: Bröderna Lagerströms förlag, 1921.

Muller, Max. *Prairie Carnegie. The Story of Presser and Ling.* Lindsborg: Quivira Press, 1977.

Myers, Robert Manson. *Handel's "Messiah." A Touchstone of Taste.* New York: MacMillan, 1948.

Oström, Alfred. "Körsånger." *Augustana.* November 7, 1901.

Perry, William Walter. " 'Messiah' Week." *New York Times,* April 2, 1950.

Powell, M. K. "Handel and Bach," *Kansas City Star,* April 18, 1935.

Prins Wilhelm, "A Swedish Oasis." *American-Scandinavian Review,* February, 1928. Pp. 103–06.

Sevärdheter i Västergötland. Skaraborgs län. Stockholm: Liber förlag, 1981.

Ship's List S. S. New York. Southhampton to New York. October 20, 1900.

Ship's List S. S. Republic. Liverpool to Boston, September 28, 1906.

Simpson, Guy Criss. "Doing the 'St. Matthew Passion'." *American Organist,* September, 1937.

Tre socknar genom tiderna. Kållands-Råda, Mellby, Åsaka. Mossebro: Rydéns tryckeri, 1970.

Turtle, Howard. "Kansas Festival." *New York Times,* March 26, 1939.

———. "Oberammergau of the Plains." *Reader's Digest,* April, 1944.

"Wheat Belt Messiah." *Time,* April 17, 1939.

Åstrand, Hans, and Larsson, Gunnar. *The Royal Swedish Academy of Music.* Stockholm: Kungl. musikaliska akademien, 1983.

INDEX

26, 1925, 77; April 4, 1929, 78; April
10, 1941, 66; May 28, 1936, 82;
March 26, 1929, 60; March 22, 1945,
69
Lindsborgs-Posten quoted March 31,
1915, 52; April 4, 1928, 60
Lindsborg Record, quoted October 12,
1906, 43; April 2, 1915, 52
Ling, Per Henrik, 126
Ling Auditorium-Gymnasium (for-
mer "Messiah" Auditorium, often
referred to in oratorio perfor-
mances prior to 1929), 58–60
Linné, Carl von, 47, 113, 126
Lofgren, Dean Oscar, 31, 58, 75, 117,
122
Lofgren, Richard, 118, 140, note 22
Lofgren, Mrs. Richard. See Brase, In-
grid
Lofgren, Ronald, 138–39, note 21
London, 27
Loveland, Colorado, Reporter-Herald,
quoted April 9, 1940, 83
Lundsbrunn, 21, 42, 109
Lundstrom, Maridene Newell, quoted
96
Luther, Martin, role of music, 76, 105,
107–08
Lützen, visit in, 24
Lächö Castle, 1, 42
Läsare, 102
McCray, Dr. Walter, 92
McPherson Daily Republican, quoted
March 17, 1942, 67
Malloy, H. C., 59
Male Chorus, conductor of, 46
Malm, Rev. Ervin C., 131
Malm, G. N., 43, 58, 60, 116, 121
Memorial Scholarship, Hagbard
Brase, 128
Martin, Roberta Pruitt, quoted 94, 100
Marysville, Kansas, 127
"Messiah" Auditorium (later Ling
Gymnasium), 58–60; final "Mes-
siah" concert, 60; celebrity con-
certs, 59–60
Messiah Lutheran Church, 131
"Messiah" performances (selected

dates of), March 28, 1915, 52; April
6, 1916, 53; April 1, 1917, 53; May
5, 1918 (100th performance), 53;
May 13, 1918 (Camp Funston), 53–
54; February 8–9, 1922 (Oklahoma
City, Oklahoma), 54–55; November 18–19, 1922 (Kansas City, Missouri), 56–57; April 8, 1928 (final
performance in old "Messiah" Auditorium), 58–60; March 24, 1929
(first performance in Presser Hall),
60–61; December 13–14, 1929
(Kansas City, Missouri), 61–62;
December 11–12, 1930 (Kansas
City, Missouri), 62; April 16, 1933,
62; April 14, 1935, 62–63; April 2,
1920, 63–64; April 12, 1938, 65;
March 11, 1934 (Wichita, Kansas),
65; April 6, 1941, 66–67; March 29–
April 5, 1942 (60th anniversary),
66–67; April 21, 1943 (performance for military personnel in
Lindsborg), 67; April 9, 1944 (dedicatory performance), 67; November 18, 1945 (Kansas City, Mis-
souri), 68; April 21, 1946 (last
performance with Hagbard Brase
as conductor), 68–69
"Messiah" tradition in Lindsborg, 51–
72
Montana, Marie, 61, 78
Morgontidningen, October 2, 1937,
quoted 26, 126
Morini, Erika, 60
Moster Sofia (Mrs. Johan Linde),
quoted 8; 19, 26, 38, 42, 43, 109–
10, 122
Muller, Max, 59
Music theory courses, 36–37, 46, 97
Music in church. See entry "Church
Music"
Music, view of, 76, 92, 105, 107
Musical America, quoted April 25,
1941, 66
Musical Courier, quoted May 10, 1938,
65
Music News, quoted November 5,
1915, 99